THE RIVER
WITHIN
心中的河流

THE RIVER WITHIN

Wang Ping

MadHat Press
Cheshire, Massachusetts

MadHat Press
MadHat Incorporated
PO Box 422, Cheshire, MA 01225

Copyright © 2023 Wang Ping

The Library of Congress has assigned this edition a Control Number of 2023947395

ISBN 978-1-952335-68-6 (paperback)

Words by Wang Ping
Book design by MadHat Press
Cover design by Marc Vincenz
Cover photo by Adam Stoltman
Cover calligraphy by Su Hongqing
Author photo by Jinn Bug

www.madhat-press.com

First Printing
Printed in the United States of America

The book is dedicated to

The Mississippi River and all the rivers on earth. You gave me life, inspiration, wisdom, peace and happiness;

To Gary Snyder, who dedicated his whole being to rivers and mountains.

Table of Contents

Part I: The River Within 心中的河流

My Mississippi 我的密西西比	3
Why I Row Ten Thousand Meters Every Day 我为什么每天划艇一万米	6
Third Eye 天眼	7
Entropy—熵	11
Biography of Green: an edible sonnet ghazal 绿色传记：撒哈儿14行	16
Magic 神奇	19
And the Old Man Speaks of Paradise: a ghazal 老人河说天堂：哈撒儿	22
Hippocampus 海马体	26
American Sonnet 美国十四行诗	30
On the Dog Mountain 狗山	32
A Dream Is Not a Dream 流浪密西西比	36
The Music of Reeds: a ghazal 交响芦苇：哈撒儿	39
The River Has No Tongue 河流没有舌头	41
The River Within Us: a ghazal 心里的江河—哈撒儿	43
Teleportation 同传	45
Every Mammal Gets 1.5 Billion Heartbeats 每个生命都有十五亿次心跳	48
The Universe in My Bowl 碗里的宇宙	51
And the Birds Guide Us 鹤鸟为我们带路	53
Confession of a Ruby-Throat 红玉喉北蜂鸟的自白	56
Sky Earth Human 四月	61
Skin Deep 深透皮肤	65
The Language of Cephalopod 头足纲的语言	67
Things That Matter Catch Us by Surprise 重要的事总是出其不意地赶上我们	70
Turn Your Face to the Sun and Shadows Fall 把你的脸对准太阳	72
What Holds 是什么让我们飞翔	75

The Story of Stones 石头的故事 77
Jewelweed 珠草 80

Part II: Food for Gods

Food for Gods 87
Ode to Virus 89
Where the Yangtze Stands Behind the Three Gorges Dam 92
Everest—After Passing Three Checkpoints without a Permit 93
October Snow: for Amy from Georgia 94
Fox 96
Highway 61 97
Crab and Catfish 99
Donald Judd's Secret Paradise in Mafa 101
The Instinct to Swarm 102
Oracle 104
The Meridian Gate 105
Eudemonia 107
Jewel of the Himalaya 110
This Is My Garden 112

Part III

Jerusalem, Jerusalem 耶路撒冷，耶路撒冷 119

Part IV: How a Droplet Becomes a Tsunami

How a Droplet Becomes a Tsunami: Field Notes from Standing Rock 131

Part V: The River in Our Blood: Sonnet Crown to Lord Bruce 血液里的河流：十四行诗皇冠

Sonnet I	十四行I	148
Sonnet II	十四行II	150
Sonnet III	十四行III	152
Sonnet IV	十四行IV	154
Sonnet V	十四行V	156
Sonnet VI	十四行VI	158
Sonnet VII	十四行VII	160
Sonnet VIII	十四行VIII	162
Sonnet IX	十四行IX	164
Sonnet X	十四行X	166
Sonnet XI	十四行XI	168
Sonnet XII	十四行XII	170
Sonnet XIII	十四行XIII	172
Sonnet XIV	十四行XIV	174
Sonnet Crown	十四行皇冠	176

Acknowledgments 181
About the Author 183

Part I
The River Within
心中的河

心中的河流 THE RIVER WITHIN

My Mississippi

In the beginning
there is a berry—manoomin—wild & good
rice in water, a harvest for bugs, fish, birds …
before men, before there was a gorge
ploughed by River Warren, the Forgotten River
remembered by black soil and ten thousand lakes
its glacial water pushing Minnehaha Fall backwards
through the Twin Cities—my home
on the cliff, watching two rivers murmur, converge
watching you freeze overnight, misty clouds galloping
white buffalos into my dreams
on your icy skin, along your curving spine
trees, deer, skiers, sturgeons, turtles
your pulse under whiteout swamps, sandbars
when you open your mouth in spring
I come running, with my red boat and white wings
I glide and push, my two thousand prayers
along your temple of dawn and dusk
through wind and heat, till the wheel spins
green past blue, orange, red
till you show your true color—
blood from the artery of the purple prairie
from the heart of the Turtle Island
and I become who I am
a red blood cell
a fish
a fox
a leaf returning
the big river …
my Mississippi & Yangtze

Wang Ping 王屏

我的密西西比

初始
只是一粒种子——玛弩泯——野米，好米
站在水里的米，养育着虫，鱼，鸟，树木…
那时没有人类，也没有河谷
只有沃伦古冰川河，被遗忘的河
嵌入黑土和湖泊的记忆
沉重的冰划开了双子城
逼着米妮哈哈瀑布后退几十里
我的家就在悬崖峭壁上
最喜欢你的一夜冰封，千里江河
只剩下白雾奔腾
如野牛在梦里横冲直撞
沿着你七里一弯的脊梁
行走的森林，麋鹿，河豚，乌龟，大雁
还有在你洁白皮肤上滑雪的人类
幻想如何主宰冰层湿地下的脉搏
春天你刚开口，还来不及呼叫
我就举着红船白桨冲上你的舌尖
两千次桨声，两千个祈祷
沿着你清晨傍晚流荡
沿着你风雨阳光的的寺庙
沿着你的红狐灰鹤白头鹰
直到彩轮把翠绿推过
深蓝橘黄赤红
直到你献出你的本色——
那紫色平原大动脉的血
那跳动的龟岛之心
我终于回到我的本来——
一颗红血球　一条鱼　一只狐狸　一片回家的落叶

心中的河流 THE RIVER WITHIN

我的密西西比
我梦中的长江

1. 玛弩泯：印第安人的圣米，也叫野米，好米，丰收米，生长在密西西比源头沼泽地的湖泊里，营养丰富，是中西部湖泊区的特产，对环境清洁要求很高。
2. 沃伦古冰川河：古冰川几百万年曾覆盖整个北美中西部，融化时，冰水形成沃伦河，冲击出众多的湖泊，包括密西西比，可以说沃伦河是密西西比河的母亲，现在的明尼苏达河，沦落为污染最严重的河流，并且沾满了历史上白人屠杀印第安人的鲜血。
3. 龟岛：印第安人神话中的伊甸园。

Wang Ping 王屏

Why I Row Ten Thousand Meters Everyday

For the patrol at dawn: Is everything OK
Silverbacks, red foxes, gray cranes
Clouds, light, wind from all directions?
For my thoughts, my morning prayers
For the wings to let my dreams fly at night
For my boat filled with the Mississippi
For the Mississippi carrying a boatful of joy
I offer my boat and river to the sky
My joy takes me all the way down the Gulf

我为什么每天划艇1万米

为了第一个向黎明道早安
你好：银鲤，红狐，灰鹤
你好：日出、云、东南风
让那1万米长的冥思晨祷
把夜晚织成梦的七彩翅膀
为抹去老人河脸上的皱褶
把满河乡愁收进我的船仓
为把密西西比河举上天空
让欢喜带我漂入墨西哥湾

Third Eye

It's mid-April. A blizzard arrives with hail and sounds of chimes.

Robins have begun their flight to the north, following the smell of snow and rain, the thawing earth, and worms' vertical migration.

On her 80th birthday, my mother asked if I'd go home one more time.

A brainstorm in soft simplicity, a debate if I should become a citizen after three decades of wandering in America.

A friend sent me "The Third Snow" by Yevgeny Yevtushenko, a century-old poem from Siberia.

Blizzard is indifferent to space or time.

Still want to go back to China, asked Gary Snyder. *Aren't you on their list?*

Via WeChat, my brother marvels at my home in St. Paul, how affordable compared to his 6-million Yuan apartment, a hole on an island. He's willing to forgo the breeze from the East China Sea for a place in Minnesota freeze.

Yesterday I rowed 15k in my single scull. Today the Mississippi moans again under ice.

Yet robins know how to wait. They know when spring rides the cold front, when worms awaken the earth. They follow the 37° isotherm during their flight between Guatemala and Minnesota.

I applied for citizenship three times, but chickened out after the fingerprints. I never showed up for the swearing.

For 30 years, my mother had tried to unlock the secret of *Dao De Jing*. She was allowed to step into the Way only after she lost her sight at 73.

I know I'm on the list. I was arrested talking to migrants in a village that is now 178 meters beneath the Three Gorges Dam.

When a blizzard blows robins off course, they fly towards the sun, following its angled light to get back on track.

Two free radicals spin in their eyes, under the blue light, like two lovers, radiant with joy—this is their quantum coherence—

Our inner compass through each blizzard, forever pointing towards home.

天眼

四月，最后一场暴风雪，中部平原白茫茫一片，只有风铃在冰雪里呼喊。

知更鸟已从南方上路，沿着雨雪的气味，沿着蚯蚓垂直的蠕动，沿着融化的大地，回家。

87岁的母亲，问我啥时候回去。

流浪天涯已经三十六年，却始终剪不断那条柔软的脐带。

朋友寄给我叶夫根尼·叶夫图申科 的《第三场雪 》，来自西伯利亚的诗歌，快一百年了。

中西部的大雪，总是如此随意地抹去时空。

还想回去啊？老诗人斯奈德问我。你不是被拘留过吗？

微信视频里，弟弟看到了我的菜园，花园，房间。太便宜啦，他惊呼！

昨天我在密西西比河划单艇一万米，今天河面又结了冰。

知更鸟知道如何等待，知道春天何时乘坐寒流来临，蚯蚓何时唤醒大地。

它们沿着37度等温线，飞翔瓜地马拉与明州之间。

我三次申请公民，三次退出宣誓仪式。我无法忍受充斥宪法的虚伪。

Wang Ping 王屏

母亲花了三十年解读易经，直到她73岁失明后，才涉入道的河流。

当暴风把知更鸟吹出飞行轨道，它们便朝着太阳飞翔，顺着斜斜的光线，重入归途。

它们的双眼间，有一对游离基，如同情侣，在蓝光下，发出欢乐的光芒，这就是它们的量子相干—

是我们内在的指南，无论穿越多少次暴风雪，永远永远指向老家。

心中的河流 THE RIVER WITHIN

Entropy 熵

"Happy families are all alike," so begins Anna Karenina.
Life is a bitch, oops, a fish out of water. Entropy rules us
like a tyrant, no, a sage: anything that can go wrong,
will go wrong. Beautiful Anna, her passion burns
in a disarray of entropy—熵—bush fire at the foot of
mountains—an oracle from China, 1000 years ago.
忌—misfortunes begin with the heart, tied by desire
at birth. So thin is the path to happiness, weeps Anna,
thinner than the blade in a storm of bullets. Time moves
in the manner of arrow. 忌—a heart tied down with ropes
by our own hands. We remembered yesterday, and how
Anna began her story. Yet who remembered her tomorrow,
or the fate of the physicist dreaming of the particle—
half angel, half demon? Beauty happens in a miracle,
our dreams, so fragile against the teeth of entropy—twin
sisters of 忌 & 熵. Who can say we're free from Murphy's
law? Everything that can go wrong, will go wrong!
Crazed Anna, crushed under the wheels of fire—熵—
her passion just as noble as the physicist calling
for a better world, as he crashed through the window.
The train of thoughts churns as Anna flings into her own
story. She knows she has no chance to piece happiness
together, but…In China, entropy comes with fire—熵—
mother of ash. Without burning or rotting, the mountain
shall have no earth. In science, order comes out of chaos,
always. Entropy—shang—a world rhyming with 墒—
moist soil, then 殇—a child dead before grown up,
a physicist flung out of his own dreams, and Anna,
sacrificed for the order of family, for negentropy,
anti-chaos, anti-matter. "If you leave now,

Wang Ping 王屏

you'll regret for the rest of your life," said my ex.
No, Anna never had a chance for love,
in the grip of order, the family machine
designed to strangle. "I know I'll regret it,
but I have to go," I said, walking out of the mansion.
So Anna enters, alone with a naked heart,
her beauty is a mirror from another kingdom.
All that should be burnt, will burn, so life can start again
from zero, predicted I-jing, a thousand years ago.
Tolstoy wrote the story to teach a lesson about
the tyranny of Entropy, its twin sister ji 忌—ropes
around joy. "Every unhappy family is unhappy
in its own way," he murmurs, as he throws Anna
under the train to show us the horror.
Who's Anna, who's the physicist, carrying
so much beauty under the sun, as he decoded
the universe from a grain of sand, with Blake's vision?
Are we nothing but aliens, trying to make sense
of humanity through a quantum highway of passion?
Are we mere fish in a dry bucket, a sandcastle
in tsunami, never supposed to win this mismatched war?
Yet we keep flinging ourselves under the train,
keep breathing through our lungs
after we lost our gills, growing our own crops
after banished from the Garden. We spin one miracle
after another, to keeps Anna's story alive, our dreams,
our poetry and failure, especially our failure—
熵 & 忌—fire burning down the ropes
so the heart keeps singing
as a proof of our existence

a firebird out of
shang—熵—entropy.

熵

"幸福的家庭都一模一样。"
就这样，安娜卡列妮娜展开了自己的故事。
生活是条狗，哦错了，是搁浅的鱼。
熵缠绕着我们,如圣者的诅咒:
所有会出事的地方，都会出事。
美丽的安娜，她的激情，比熵更疯狂。

贲：山火，一千多年前的预言，烧上
2021年的西山。 一切的不幸，都来自
心头的纠结——忌。而通往幸福的路,
只有一条。哭泣的安娜，她知道，
自己的命运，比刀刃还要单薄。
时间的箭头，为什么总是射向未来？
我们都记得过去，可谁在安娜故事的开头，
就记住了她惨烈的明天？谁还记得
张首晟的粒子：一半天使，一半魔鬼？

忌——人心，竟被自己的绳结捆死。
所有的美丽都是奇迹。我们的梦，
在熵的齿间，多么弱小、无力。
忌——熵，这对孪生姐妹，
把我们的生生死死，缠在
墨菲定律的法轮：任何会出错的，都会出错！

Wang Ping 王屏

痴迷的安娜，就这样，
被熵的轮子，辗得粉碎。
她对爱的追求，与物理学家的天使宇宙，
一样高尚。而命运，也平等地
把他们一起抛出窗外。
小说开始启动，安娜毫不犹豫地
跳进故事的车厢，虽然她知道，
完成幸福这个拼图，已不可能。

象形文字的熵，带着火部——
这是不是意味，熵，竟然是大地的母亲！
没有腐烂和燃烧，山就不会有土。
而科学，把混乱的熵，视为秩序的源泉。
Entropy——熵，通墒，燃烧后的土地，
终于得到滋润。熵，通殇——早夭的孩子，
战死的士兵，被抛出窗外的诺贝尔候选人，
还有安娜，她美丽的身体，被用来
祭奠家庭的秩序和负熵。

"今天你走出这个大门，会后悔一辈子，"
前夫警告我。在家庭的熵里，安娜有过
爱的机会吗？"我知道我会后悔,但是，"
我回答，昂着头走出了大门。
就这样，安娜把一颗赤子之心，
嵌入另一面世界的镜子。

无妄，明夷，贲——该烧的都将烧尽，
只留下一张素纸，描画新的纪元。
预言，为什么只能向前？
一千年前的古人，怎么会记住，

心中的河流 THE RIVER WITHIN

12万9千年后的故事？
托尔斯泰怎么知道忌与熵的
暴力和温柔？他一边喃喃自语，
"每一个不幸的家庭都有自己的故事，"
一边把安娜抛向前进的列车。

我们是历史浅滩上的鱼，
海啸脚下的沙堡。
但安娜竟敢用生命，换取爱情！
顶着太阳的物理学家，竟然
用布莱克的诗歌，探索宇宙的秘密，
让混乱的人性之熵，整齐地进入量子公路！
注定会失败的安娜，为什么如此光彩明艳？
海洋生物，为什么爬上陆地，学会用肺呼吸？
我们创造奇迹，创造安娜、天使、魔鬼，
创造梦，诗歌，
还有一次又一次的失败——

我们的忌与熵，
我们生命的烈火，
烧尽捆绑我们的绳索，
让火鸟冲出焦土，
让心，跳得更加沉稳、自主。

Wang Ping 王屏

Biography of Green: an Edible Sonnet Ghazal

With fiddle hands, I fold & unfold light, painting air with emerald green
Turning CO_2 into sugar + O, till I drape the Earth with 24 shades of green

This planet was born in a ball of fire, then basalt, then granite, then glacial ice
With sleight of hand, I pickled her into lime, sage, basil, pear and apple green

I tap, clap, spin, whisper, sway with willows, my juniper veins open to the sun
My moss blood running toward roots, and life sings with parakeet green

Awakened from arctic dreams, I chase grassland and forests with seaweed tendrils
A linchpin between sky & earth, my wavelength paints cypress with spruce green

Spectrum between blue and yellow, Rosetta Stone for fern, shamrock, seafoam
Sitting amidst the rainbow wheel, I open seasons with chartreuse mustard green

Chinese make no difference between blue & green; they say 青出于蓝必胜于蓝
So let green=chlorophyll=photosynthesis=O=glucose=pear=pine=ocean green

A cycle without beginning or end, my sapphire waves
    shimmering, lighting up
First word, smell, taste, sound, touch … till Earth hangs on a
    twig of olive green

Count pollens on cypress, count hands on aspen trees, count
    trees on Earth
Behold Earth in my 120 quadrillion leaves, a Panthalassa of
    pistachio green

绿色传记：撒哈儿14行

你用奏响琴弦的手，折叠展开光线，把空气抹成翠绿
以二氧化碳转换氧气蔗糖，直到大地披上二十四层绿

先是火球，然后是玄武岩球，花岗岩球，古冰川球
你的巧手把地球腌成酸橙，蓬蒿，鼠尾草，苹果绿

你轻叩，击掌，旋转，柳枝杜松的脉络，朝太阳开放
青苔里的血脉，直通树根，直至生命唱起鹦歌祖母绿

从北极梦中醒来，你用海苔的卷须追逐草原森林
夹持天地，你的波长为青竹圈起层层水杉薄荷绿

坐在蓝黄之间，罗塞塔石解开蕨类，三叶草的秘密
乘着彩虹色谱轮，你开启四季，让鹅黄掺上芥末绿

Wang Ping 王屏

把世间的所有的绿,穿过日照、叶绿素,合成果糖
青出于蓝必胜于蓝,千里江山,万顷松海,如此蓝绿

无始无终的循环,蓝宝石波遥遥闪闪点燃一个绿字
一口气、一个声音、一次触觉,让星球挂满橄榄绿

数不清的松柏花粉,拍不够的杨树叶,穿不透的热带雨林
把蓝色星球捧在你120万亿片掌心,泛古洋一片开心果绿

Magic

Birds sing because they have a song in their throats
Fish swim because they have an ocean in their bellies
The wind blows to play with the rivers and valleys
Raindrops fall as messengers upon the earth
We move with the dance in our spirits
Children run as the world unfolds under their feet

This is the secret of magic
Hidden in our brains
The people and their small things
If all taken away, what would we miss?
The rustle of oak trees at dusk
The foaming river outside the window
The smell of children coming home
Cheeks red from the snow
The little thing you say that's not funny
But I laugh anyway just because …

The birds can't be imitated
The flowers can't be colored
The sea can't be dammed
The mountains can't be conquered

This is the sound of magic
Running in our veins
Moving the sky and earth
Passing through us like rivers
All the noise on earth will die
But not this silence of faith

Wang Ping 王屏

This innocence persisting to believe
To see more than what can be seen

神奇

鸟儿引颈高歌，是为了喉咙深处的曲子
鱼儿畅游深蓝，是为了腹中的大海
风飘来飘去，为寻找河流山谷玩耍
雨点来到大地，为我们传达宇宙的信息
我们舒展腰肢，为了表达心中的舞蹈
孩子们奔跑，让世界在他们的脚下绽放

这就是神奇的秘密
潜卧在我们的心底
假如没有亲人和他们的琐事
我们还剩什么？
黄昏时橡树的唏嘘
窗外吐着白沫的河流
孩子们回家时的满头大汗
冰雪冻得通红的脸颊
你问我那些零碎小事
为什么让我开怀大笑
那是因为

鸟儿无法被模仿
花儿无法被描绘
大海无法被阻拦
雪山无法被征服

那神奇的声音

心中的河流 THE RIVER WITHIN

在我们的血液里流淌
它可以感天动地
如河流穿越我们的心灵
人间的尘埃最终都会落地
而这沉默的信念
不断地替我们指点
肉眼看不见的神奇

Wang Ping 王屏

And the Old Man Speaks of Paradise: a ghazal

Do not move. Let me speak of a river in paradise
A turquoise gift from fiery stars—that is paradise

How do you measure a river's weight, color, smell, touch?
How do you feel the veins of sand in a breathing paradise?

Eons of earth story, long before rocks, plants or bones
Bulging with flesh and blood in every corner of paradise

You call me Old Man, 12,000 years old, but really, I'm a baby of
River Warren, swollen with glacier water flooding the paradise

My torso sloughed by old ice, two cities on sandstone bluffs
Headwaters of a 2350-mile road towards the gulf of paradise

A walk along the beach, a bag of rocks, fossils and agates
Each tells stories of river, land & life—a kinship of paradise

Come at dawn by foot, canoe or single shell. Meet my children:
Eagles, foxes, beavers, trees ... a ten-mile gorge of paradise

And walleye, redhorse, gar, stoneroller, stickleback, drum, bass
Mooneye, buffalo, bowfin, sunfish, darter ... in the wave of
    paradise

And St. Anthony Fall walking 10 miles upriver from Fort
    Snelling
Clams and shells in Kasota stones—a layered history of
    paradise

心中的河流 THE RIVER WITHIN

Put your fingers into the bluff, and pull a handful of sand
From the Ordovician sea, each perfect to make a paradise

From time to time, I take you into the amniotic womb
A reminder of our origin from a black, red, white, blue paradise

Do not dam me. To move freely is to evolve is to thrive
Locks feed fear feed hate feed violence to the base of paradise

The Mississippi, temple on Earth, home of all living things
Would you tread with love, through the heart of paradise?

We are water—H_2O—two hands cradling an open heart
Pulsing, dissolving, bonding the Earth to a green paradise

Stop seeking before or after life, for a paradise already
Within us, each cell of sentient being—that is paradise

老人河说天堂：哈撒儿

别动。让我说，有一条大河，流出天堂
宝蓝的太空礼物—你能说，那不是天堂？

你如何测量河的体重、肤色、气味、触觉？
你可听见热胀冷缩的沙粒，怎样呼吸天堂？

Wang Ping 王屏

地球的初世纪，没有岩石、植物、骨头
更无生命的血肉，涨满边边角角的天堂

你叫我老人，一万二千岁，可我只是个孩子
母亲叫沃伦古河，冰川融化的水，淹没天堂

古冰冲涮我的躯体，砂岩峭壁上，站起双子城
两千三百五十英里，从北方奔向墨西哥湾天堂

沿着我的沙滩行走，捡起一把石头，化石、玛瑙
每个故事，都是河流、土地、生命——细数天堂

黎明前来见我的孩子吧，光脚，带上独木舟、划艇
白头鹰，红狐，水獭，灰鹤，嬉戏十里河谷的天堂

更有那玻璃梭鲈、红马、滚石、镰背、太阳鱼
鲈鱼、月眼、野牛鲤、亚洲银鲤，飞跃龙门天堂

圣安东尼瀑布，从斯奈凌碉堡倒退十英里
嵌在卡索塔黄石里的贝壳，露出层层天堂

五指插入悬崖，抓一把奥陶世纪的沙土
每一粒如此金黄灿烂，造就完美的天堂

每隔一段时间，我带你进入生命的子宫
重温地球由黑到红、白、来到蔚蓝天堂

别挡我。流淌是生命演化的需求
大坝锁住洪水灾难，也锁住天堂

心中的河流 THE RIVER WITHIN

密西西比河，地球的寺庙，万物的源泉
愿你带着爱，轻轻地淌过我心底的天堂

我们都是水——H_2O——捧着赤裸的心
拍打、融化，让世界汇流成翠绿天堂

别去前生后世寻寻觅觅，天堂已坐在
我们心中，每个细胞，都是一个天堂

注：
这首哈撒儿，受美国国家公园庆祝100周年委员会邀请而写。我的家在圣保罗崖壁上，对岸是斯奈凌碉堡，明尼苏达河（也是古沃伦河）在此与密西西比汇合，两岸十英里的峭壁，是密西西比唯一的河谷，有着独特的地理现象，是国家公园的重点保护区。我有幸住在国家公园里，每天沿河跑步、划船、滑雪滑冰、拍照、捡化石，记录地质的变更、大河的四季、历史的变换，欣赏生命的美，中西部人的朴实，我的感恩比河更宽更长。

Wang Ping 王屏

Hippocampus

Seat of memories
for yesterday, today and tomorrow,
the only part of the brain
that keeps growing or shrinking.
It's a needle
sewing the past and future together,
A handful of threads
weaving reality into silk brocade.
"Use or lose it," says the neurologist.
If we don't recall or reinvent our pain, fear,
anger or sorrow, how do we find our joy?
Without joy, how do we seek humanity?
Without humanity, where do we stand?
And how the instance of now holds onto the future?
Handsome H.M., he lost his hippocampus to live
a "normal life," only to be tossed into the sea of present tense,
drifting between hospital and lab, from one event to another,
forever now and here, but no yesterday.
Where is that young gentle Henry?
Who is this good old HM without a story?
Homo sapiens experts tell us:
the size of hippocampus is the key for memory—
foundation for logic and emotions that allow us
to plan our future, the hallmark separating us from beasts.
But how do we explain elephants carrying
the biggest memory house for smell, sound, touch and love?
And chimps, who play politics better than the baboons in the
White House?
And the crows who remember faces and know what to do
with friends or enemies?

Monarchs who remember every milkweed to stay alive along
its migration route?
We think we know, as priests, professors, scientists and
conquerors …
But do we know what we don't know?
Do we hear Gaia's weeping for our sufferings?
Do we see animals laughing and watching from their
kingdoms
How we scheme our escape from this wheel of memories?
How we try to untangle ourselves from this spoke of time and
space?

海马体

第一次把人脑捧在手里,教授指着海马体说:"我们所有的故事,都在这里。"

从生到死
记忆的宝座
是大脑唯一
不断变化、生长的部位
它是一根针
把过去与未来缝合
它是一把丝线
把现实绣成锦缎

"用进废退",脑科专家说。
失去了回忆,我们如何去升华

Wang Ping 王屏

永无休止的恐惧、愤怒、爱情和痛苦？
没有升华，我们怎么落地归根？
怎么抵达人的本性？没有人性
我们何去何从？诺大的宇宙
我们如何靠现在的一瞬，抓住未来的边缘？

年轻的亨利渴望摆脱癫痫
摘除了海马体
从此被抛进现在进行时
永远的第一次见面、告别
永远的第一口尝试，永远的
惊讶悲伤，永远的这里和今天
英俊的亨利，你迷失在哪里？
没有海马的肢体
你的晚年还剩什么故事？

智力专家告诉我们
指姆般大的海马体，是保存记忆的关键
记忆的多少，是情感理智的钥匙
而运用理智，是划分人与动物的根本
但我们如何解释大象？
她们对嗅觉声音和抚摸的记忆，她们慈爱的突触
为什么远超人类？每年飘飞万里的帝王斑蝶
怎么算得出路上每一株维持生命的乳汁草？
为什么乌鸦可以分辨人的嘴脸，拿我们的怪癖习俗
判断意图的黑白？大猩猩高超的政治手腕
是白宫政客的必学之课，为什么世界还是战火不断？

人畜之间的红线，到底划在哪里
那红线，真的是海马也无法跨越的深渊？

28

心中的河流 THE RIVER WITHIN

我们以为知道一切
自称是征服地球的主宰
却不知我们多么无知不幸
而动物在自己的王国里嘻嘻笑着
看我们如何逃脱记忆的牢笼
如何被时空轮回缠住

注释

H. M. Henry Malaison, 亨利马莱森, 1926–2008, 27岁时,因严重的癫痫做了切脑手术,摘除了海马体,失去了把现今的体验和信息转换成记忆的能力,从而生活无法自理,一生住在医院里,成为脑科研究最珍贵的第一手资料,为大脑神经,记忆,学习和人性的研究,作出了巨大的贡献。

Frans De Waal 弗朗斯德瓦尔的《大猩猩的政治:权利与性》,美国从事政治的,人手一册,但似乎都读反了,因为大猩猩的最终目的,是避免战争和暴力,以性,社交与其他的方式,用最少流血的代价,去维持权利,保证群体的生存。

Wang Ping 王屏

American Sonnet

If blessing is a transfer of energy
Is story a needle through our memory?

Elms, hands, sonnets … passing through a birchbark prairie
A train glides into a whiteout campus of downtown St. Paul

Cajons, hand drums, dumplings for the Year of the Pig
No entry before 5:00, and everyone out by 6:30, says the
    liberal chaplain

Who could foresee the lies plaguing our eyes and hearts?
Only good thoughts please, pleads the Chinese poet, for all
    sentient beings

On New Year's Day and every day, till our brain rewires itself
    into a love nest
Students cheer when Good Heart walks in, drum on his back,
    blizzard in his hair

If matter is energy, which wave or particle or song awakens
    our souls?
What love makes our limbs tremble like wings of luna moth?

What hand threads the story from finger to finger, mouth to
    mouth
Till each word is pregnant with fruits of memory and blessing?

美国十四行诗

假如祝福是能量的转移,我们的故事
难道不正在为我们的记忆穿针引线?

榆树,手,涂鸦,火车穿过白桦树平原
慢慢驶进圣保罗大雪纷飞的校园

打着手鼓,西班牙鼓,我们在教堂包饺子过猪年
校园牧师命令:5:00前不得入内,6:30必须离开

嫉妒与仇恨,让我们成为色盲,心灵却不断
发出祝福:让所有的生灵日夜平安快乐

直到我们的大脑重新筑成幸福的鸟巢
直到印第安酋长头顶大鼓,走进学生的欢呼

哪一支歌,哪一个波粒,唤醒了我们的灵魂
欢乐让我们的四肢颤抖,如同月光娥的翅膀

双手编织故事,一针一线
让记忆,载起满满的祝福

Wang Ping 王屏

On Dog Mountain of Oregon

Sunflowers bloom in fury
Wind presses them against steep slopes
In 50 mph gusts, they sway and bend and laugh
Spitting golden pollen into the blue
The meadow is saturated, and the forest below
Aquiver with green, yellow, cream mists

> Pollen grain is not a male gamete but potential
> Bamboo is not a tree but a blade of grass

Along the Columbia and sacred Wind Mountain
The Multnomah Fall flowed from a father's sorrow
After his daughter jumped to break the smallpox rampage
Dog Mountain belongs to coyotes, bears, and spirits
The history of first nations lives in books and internets
Their legends in shadows of the Big Foot, a few names
Here and there: Multnomah, Klickitat, Chinook …
Their spirits blown in the wind
Pollinating mountains, rivers and Columbia Gorge

> In the high wind, through a bee's knees
> Pollens gain footholds in pistils
> Its cells splitting into a flower, a fruit, a seed
> a tree, a meadow, a forest

Young men bring their dates to the Dog Mountain
To watch how their beloved climb and hug the slope
Their body bending and swaying like a blade of bamboo
Their sweat in the howling wind

心中的河流 THE RIVER WITHIN

How large is a grain of pollen?
Look at the Marvel of Peru
Blooming at 4 o'clock
Roots four feet into rocks

In pine forests, pollens grow wings
Green moss shimmers through perforated light
And streams sing over pebbles and boulders
Love bounces from cone to cone, petal to petal
Tree to tree, as bees wallow in the sea of yellow
Like submarines, as forget-me-nots send out
Troops of smallest love-knots to split hearts

    Tread the meadow with care
    In each blade of grass
    Lurks a name, a tear, a seed of memory

A mature ovary is a fruit
A mature ovule becomes a seed

    On the Dog Mountain
    Sunflowers dance in hurricane wind

Wang Ping 王屏

狗山

每小时50英里的风，把葵花
按在陡坡。太阳花笑着
金色的花粉，喷向蓝天
山腰下，团团的松果
在乳黄暗绿的花雾里招手

摇旖的翠竹不是树，只是一根杂草
花粉不是雄性配子，而是一种潜能

狗山不是山，是熊、土狼的家
酋长的女儿莫娜马，为阻挡
天花的蔓延，跳进风里祭祖
父亲的眼泪流成一条瀑布
印第安人从此销声匿迹
他们的名字残留在野人的脚印
莫娜马、克里基塔、奇努克⋯

狂风里，蜂鸟铮铮的翅膀
为哥伦比亚大峡谷授粉

男子带着情侣攀爬狗山
汗水渗进嚎叫的风
情人四肢拥抱陡坡的模样
比青竹更抚媚妖娆

花粉的颗粒有多么宏大？
秘鲁的神奇，月亮花、夜美人
根，直插岩石四尺，下午四点
红蓝黄绿的花，按时占领山头

心中的河流 THE RIVER WITHIN

花粉多么细小？
紫花地丁散发的配子—勿忘我多么
精致可爱，其根，可以钻地三尺
芳草坡上，雌芯张开茸茸的花房
蜜蜂似黄色潜艇，在花海里纵情

向日葵拍风狂舞
青苔闪烁，松林隐隐约约

分裂子宫，先醉倒在花芯
花粉深入花房—细胞裂变
子房溢满汁蜜
成花，成果，成树林和山川
而卵巢以坚硬的心，成熟了种子

行走在狗山的花丛
请步步小心
每一片花瓣草叶
沾满精魂

注释
2017年，我受加拿大几所大学的邀请，漂流哥伦比亚河，从加拿大源头哥伦比亚湖一直到俄勒冈洲入海口阿斯托里亚，沿河做"江河缘"装置艺术。到了俄勒冈州的峡谷，我攀上狗山，这里以强风、陡坡、小葵花著名。脚下，哥伦比亚河绕狗山大转弯，无比壮丽。此地原属印第安莫娜马、克里基塔，奇努克等土著人的领地，被白人以武力和天花灭族。

Wang Ping 王屏

A Dream Is Not a Dream

What makes a woman smile
Her dimples open like butterflies?
What makes a carp leap over the rainbow?
Or rivers thunder from another ether?

A turtle climbs all day up to the cliff
Only to plummet again into the river
A spinning shaman calls out to heaven
Lifting the earthlings to stars

Our temple of copper, stones and cedars
Our pond of fish, frogs, and lotus blossom
Our game of go, black and white
Our thoughts across the impossible chasm

After ten thousand strokes
My hands know the oars
After ten million dips
My oars know the water
And my water knows the shore
That knows the sound of crickets
Through long voluptuous nights

A dream is not a dream
At every bend an eagle awaits
The river offers no service or mercy
The great blue heron leads our way

心中的河流 THE RIVER WITHIN

流浪密西西比

什么风,吹开少女的嘴唇
让酒窝,旋出蜻蜓的翅膀

什么云,诱银鲤跳过彩虹
让河水,在另一以太歌唱

谁的梦,驱使河龟攀黄石悬崖
到达顶峰后,又一头摔回河底

谁的旋律,让巫师旋转呼叫星空
推芸芸众生摆脱引力,进入天穹

下游的南方,冬夜依旧丰满
独木舟,划不透两岸的秘密

穿过了弯弯曲曲的宽窄水道
小船,仍未尝遍世间的五味

从北源到南尾,全程密西西比
我的手,终于合上双桨的节奏

谁投下神秘的种子?一夜间
温和慈祥的老人,冰封千里

鹭鸶举起双翅,托着梦回家
河床不挽留怜悯、只送爱情

这是我的家乡——梦中的鱼、鸟、松林
这是我的棋盘——黑子、白子包抄世界

Wang Ping 王屏

这是我的祈祷——冲出密不透风的黑洞
这是我的寺庙——蓝天灌顶，绿水铸身

心中的河流 THE RIVER WITHIN

The Music of Reeds: a Ghazal

The wind bends and bends me into New Year's ice
Next comes the sun, stretching my bones across ice

It's below zero. In the lake, molecules trembling
Await the first seed, to form an instant sheet of ice

Tracks of fox across the frozen lake ... children jump
with dogs, ice huts rising like ghosts at the edge of ice

My flesh and spirits, blown here and there. From naked
Trees, a murder of crows caws, shattering the heart of ice

Every frozen footprint defines us, within, without
A blessing is transfer of light, in the forest of ice

Who sees us, shadow, light, curious eyes?
What voice awakens us from stone, woods & ice?

This is my spine of music, buried and alive
A symphony—molten through a bed of ice

Wang Ping 王屏

芦苇交响曲：哈撒儿

怒号的风，吹断我的腰，把我浸入湖底
接着来了太阳，把我的骨头，拉成瘦冰

水温早已降过零点，倔强的水分子
颤抖着等待第一颗冰种，瞬间成冰

冬天占领水域，冻结狐狸精致的脚印
狼狗拉着孩子们，围绕冰屋嬉戏滑冰

我的灵魂与肉体，随风呼啸飘摇湖面
秃树群鸦，声声凄厉，震碎湖心的冰

白雪里的脚印，映衬我们里外的轮廓
祝福是光的传递，照亮丛林起伏的冰

谁看见我们，阴影，光线，惊讶的眼睛？
什么声音把我们唤醒——石头，树木，冰？

这是音乐的脊椎，埋葬、呼吸
一曲交响——敲开湖底千年的冰

The River Has No Tongue

A starving waif pulses from the window screen
Wei cries his heart out for his stolen I-phone
My fingers type out thoughts filling the air with pellets of rain
Across the river, a lover cuts open a bleeding orange

At the window my face opens to the mid-winter sun
Heavy doses of Vitamin D to calm inflamed keloids
The Mississippi is half frozen half open
Dogs and skiers move on the ice with a heart-wrenching grace

We seek fire to ignite the universe
We summon darkness to fight demons
The rivers meet and curve around the bend
Our paths crisscross, but never touch

Deep in the snow, trees stand naked
A silent vow unleashes its wings
Who says memory has no soul?
See how it extends its roots, bone to bone

A woodpecker calls from the abandoned tepee
A lotus blooms through the mirror of ice
The river has no tongue
Fish and turtles roam with raven spirits

Wang Ping 王屏

河流没有舌头

有个精灵,在风雨中敲打窗檐
有个孩子,为丢失的苹果手机抽泣
有双手,敲打键盘,天空就下起冰雹
有一把刀,在河的对岸,为情人划开血橘

打开天窗,我把脸伸进冬至的太阳
我们用维他命D,扑灭瘢痕瘤的怒火
密西西比河,一半冻结,一半流淌
麋鹿群沿岸奔跑,优雅得让人哭泣

我们到处寻找火种,点亮宇宙
睡眠里招魂,把噩梦挡在门外
河流蜿蜒,汇合,然后分开
盘山小路上,我们总是擦肩而过

白桦林站在雪里,赤身裸体
古老的誓言在空中飞来飞去
海马体被连根拔起
根须交错的记忆,横躺大地

啄木鸟扣击印第安人遗弃的帐篷
冰河如镜,唯有莲花开放
河流不再说话
鱼借着乌鸦的精魂,在冰下游荡

心中的河流 THE RIVER WITHIN

The River Within Us: A Ghazal

In my throat, the sea is brewing a storm of blood
Mountains' braided fingers, will there be blood?

Dantian—burning earth below my navel
Memory along the spine—river of fossil blood

Loess bluffs smoldering with Permian dust
Home—here, there, everywhere—in my blood

10,000 eyes in my palms, 10,000 hearts in the sky
10,000 wishes in a raging sea … older than blood

Give me feathers, I'll weave you wings of hope
Give me dreams, I'll build boats to cross this bleeding

Sea. Oh home, ghost on our breaths! Lingering
Prayers at each twilight, pulsing through our blood

Under our skin, a kinship of rivers
Black, white, yellow, red, brown … thicker than blood

Notes:
Dantian: place below the navel, the origin of life, source of chi in the Chinese meridian system

Loess bluffs are made with dust from the Permian period blown from around the globe then settled. The biggest and deepest loess deposit is the Yellow Plateau in China.

Wang Ping 王屏

心里的江河—哈撒儿

在我喉咙深处，大海掀起层层血
折叠大山的手指，渗出点点积血

丹田—脐眼下延绵不断的土地
记忆沿着脊骨—挖掘古化石血

黄土高原，飞扬着二叠纪的尘土
漂流泛洋，家—凝成心头的苦血

给我羽毛，为你编织希望的翅膀
给我梦想，带你寻找海底的骨血

家乡，呼吸间的幽灵！声声呼唤
徘徊黎明傍晚，重启远古的热血

掌心有一万双眼，天空有一万颗心
一万个祈祷，掀起层层被遗忘的血

我们的肤下，奔腾着大江大河
金木水火土——五色浓重如血

Teleportation

In Greek, *tele* means remote, and *port* is a harbor
to send, carry or deliver matter from A to B,
like teleporting a man from earth to moon,
without breaking him apart.
Newton's faithful shout: it's anti-gravity!
Quantum believers say it has nothing to do with the physical.
Teleportation delivers a state, a code of the man,
one particle at a time, from A to B.
If true, is love a state of mind?
If not, what code does it deliver, thousands of miles?
Why does it display such fragrance and fire?
And the heart—Is it a matter or code,
with its blood, veins and all the strings attached?
How does it move stars without lifting a finger?
What about fear, anger, hatred … magnified to destroy?
And kindness, her child named Joy—
Grown, harvested and teleported by poets
through pain and sorrow, trough persistent dreams?
What about dreams, the dark port
Where we fly, fight and cry, bodiless,
screaming to get out or pray to stay in?
Do you call it real, or just a code—
A dream that the world can't live without?
What's the code in the prayer from a child to God,
Alone at night, on her knees?
Do we need to know what's in her prayer?
No, we don't need to know what's in the package,
says the quantum physicist, just the way
Amazon delivers Santa's gifts from heaven to earth.
The postman doesn't know what's inside,

Wang Ping 王屏

Yet he brings such delight to every child.
Thus when A is teleported to B,
C will arrive, forever as a mystical original.
Holy C, this teleportation matter feels more like poetry—
its process, its light and weight, its leaps between A & B,
its manner of delivery in the speed of light,
its use of code to teleport our hope
that no force can copy, change or take away.
I'm no quantum physicist, just a self-claimed poet.
But I feel for certain,
When my heart is scanned a million times with lies
When my name and body is tasered with hypocrisy
It still teleports the same code—Love—to 7.8 billion hearts
50 pulses a minute, 1.5 billion beats for each life and
the particles that make a heart a heart.

同传

希腊语中，tele 是远程，port 是传递，
也是港湾——通过量子纠缠，把物质从A发到B,
以光速，把人从地球传到月亮，而毫发无损。
牛顿的信徒抗议：这叫反重力、反物理！
量子力学却说，这与物质无关。同传只送状态，
还有信息和意识——那么，爱是不是状态？
它用什么密码，把情感同传千里，并为之喷发
如此的芳香？而心，是物质还是意识？它的血，
怎么通过动脉，到达最微细的血管？它的弦，
如何牵住诺大的宇宙，并不动声色，移山填海，

心中的河流 THE RIVER WITHIN

穿越星辰?而我们如何解释恐惧和仇恨的传播?
又如何感受母亲,把战争与痛苦埋进土壤,
让诗人们耕耘、施肥、收割绵绵不断的梦想?
我们该如何解梦——它是真实,还是精灵的游荡?
它日夜停泊在意识的港口,让我们摆脱躯体,
去飞翔, 攀登,让我们尖叫着逃离,
或祈求留下?当孩子在深夜,揣着饥寒祷告,
她的倾诉,算不算物质?量子学家微笑着说,
这与祷告的内容无关,就像东风快递或亚马逊,
把圣诞从天堂传送到人间,邮递员无需知道,
里面装着什么,而收到礼物的孩子,还不是
高兴得吱哇乱叫?哦对了,谁都不能偷看
或扫描包裹——我们的眼睛,会改变世界的原状。
A到达B的瞬间, C就从魔术师的帽子里蹦出。
同传这只神奇的兔子,怎么越来越像诗歌——
竟把沉重和轻盈,无望与自豪,痛苦和快乐,
魔幻般地对立纠缠!那特定的文字符号,
在粒子和波浪间摇摆,产生聚变。
我说不清什么是量子。
我只是个自言自语的诗人。
我体内37.2兆的细胞元,
时时刻刻等候在意识的港湾,
以每分60次的脉搏,
以每世15亿次的跳动,
同传地球上78亿颗心。

Wang Ping 王屏

Every Mammal Gets 1.5 Billion Heartbeats

Doesn't matter if you're a blue whale, weighing 33 elephants
Or a honeybee bat—the smallest mammal on this planet

Doesn't matter if you're *Homo sapiens* shouting noble slogans
The lowly rats or American shrew moles burrowing underground

Or if you're the most hideous, most lovely creature in the world
A short-lived rabbit or a blue whale with a 200-year-old gift

Doesn't matter If you're a psychopath or Saint Teresa
If you live on streets or hide in a bubble of gated mansions

What matters is 1 billion beats for every lifetime
Birthright for each mammal, all even, all beautiful

A child hastens her heartbeats to leapfrog into adulthood
A senior slows down body's rhythms to preserve his memory

A mouse's heart must go fast to escape a cat's teeth
We slow down a sleeping heart to prolong sweet dreams

Life sings the same song, with different tempos
So says Kleiber's law, the divine equity of nature

Awakened from the American dream
I no longer know what justice means or humanity

My heart still bleeds when you spit on my name
Banning me from the heartland plowed with my heartbeats

心中的河流 The River Within

Even if my body is gone, my heart will keep going
On its own till it reaches its billion-beat destiny

Wang Ping 王屏

每个生命都有十五亿次心跳

无论你是蓝鲸，体重相当33头大象
还是蜂蝙蝠，地球上最小的哺乳动物

不管你是文明智人，整天高喊着自由
还是卑微的耗子，只会打地洞的鼩鼱

不管你极其丑陋还是人间最可爱的尤物
只活一岁的兔崽，还是寿长200的吹鲸

不管你精神分裂杀人，还是圣女特丽莎
流落街头的乞丐，还是呼风唤雨的富豪

每个哺乳动物都拥有15亿次的心跳
神灵赋予的礼物，生命的天然权力

孩子们加速心跳，越级跳入成年
老人减慢肢体的节奏以保存记忆

小鼠的心剧烈跳动，逃离猫齿利爪
睡眠中减缓的心率，摆脱噩梦无常

生命拍着各自的节奏，唱同一首歌
那是科雷波定律，还是天意的杆秤？

你可以毁灭我的身体，甚至我的意志
心继续搏动，奔往十五亿节拍的终点

The Universe in My Bowl

Today I made beef laab, a Thai dish so hot my mouth burns like inferno but my heart sings Paradiso and my hands can't stop digging into the bowl, like digging my garden in the spring, all the way to the East China Sea, my bowl brimming with homesickness and season's fruits: cauliflower, green beans, tomatoes red, yellow, green, chili peppers haunting me like mother's ghost, celery, garlic, ginger, potato, parsley, tarragon …each leaf marked by glacial soil, big bang dust, solar wind, moonlight, drizzle, sweat and prayer, finely chopped, mixed in, cooked over the fire, flowed through my mouth, down my stomach, liver, guts, back to the heart and lungs, a circling of gushing spring and bellowing happiness on the blue sea … this is my garden between chopsticks … a world between my palms … this is how I judge and love … this bowl of universe … this bowl of desire, sweat and dream … overflowing from my porcelain.

Wang Ping 王屏

碗里的宇宙

今天做了一道泰国辣牛肉，吃得舌头像燃烧的地狱，但我的心却化成天堂，我不停夹菜，如同在春天的花园里挖地，一直挖到地球对面，挖到东海群岛的家园，我的碗里盛满乡愁和四季：白的菜花，青的豆角，绿的西兰黄瓜，番茄是那么红黄绿紫，尖椒辣得像母亲的魂，缠住我的心，还有芹菜、大蒜、生姜、土豆、香芹、龙蒿……每一片都粘着古冰川沉淀的黑土，宇宙大爆发的沙尘，太阳风吹过的痕迹，一丝丝月光细雨，一滴滴夏日的汗水，一字字思乡的祈祷，全剁得细碎，拌得匀匀，炒得滚烫，合着口水下到胃肠肝胆，再回流到心扉，把希望注入涌泉，让底气张开肺叶，待发远航：这是我夹在筷子间的花园，这是我捧在手心的世界，这是我爱你的方式：所有的厨艺，所有的梦幻，全宇宙都装不下的泪水与欢喜，溢满我的碗。

心中的河流 THE RIVER WITHIN

And the Birds Guide Us

A dewdrop hangs on the lip of an orchid
A volcano rumbles in another ether

Something has hit us
And we don't know why

It's April. The prairie
Is brewing a new blizzard

Cornfields adrift in the whiteout wind
One-legged cranes darken the braided river

Rings of ice like shackles
And the sky in an origami dream

At the fork of the road I stand in blindfold
Lines of hexagrams, form of the formless

This light and shadow—it's all energy
Same difference in the field of perception

Every tomorrow has two handles
Every seed contains its own fortune

This is the truth to those who still trust
A thread so thin, unbreakable

Fire from the sea and into the sea—the Big
Island—ash from the womb of Earth

Wang Ping 王屏

Children of the rivers and mountains
We carry a dream as ancient as the cranes

Sailing across the sky, ocean and desert
Uttering a cry that's almost too human

The birds have moved on
And the fields still aquiver with their spirits

They do not think   they live
Simply   each day a small gift

鹤鸟为我们带路

一滴露水挂上兰花的唇瓣
火山，在另一个以太 轰鸣

有个东西打中了我们
却无法寻找前因后果

五月。中西部大草原
酝酿最后一场极地雪暴

玉米地，消失在乳白的天空
辫状的河里，鹤群单腿站立

冰一圈圈套上纤细的脚踝
天空又一次沉入梦的折叠

心中的河流 THE RIVER WITHIN

站在十字路口，我蒙着眼睛等待
看条条卦象，如何在无形中显形

光明与黑暗——是同等的能量
差异与相同，取决天地的视角

每一粒种子、预测生命走向
每一个明天、携带两把拉手

火山喷薄出海又回归大海——
夏威夷大岛——源于地心的热土

信仰、盲从、真理、愚昧
扯不断的牵连，模糊的红线

大江大河的子孙后代
我们的梦，同鹤一样古老

飞过天空，海洋，沙漠
它们的呼唤，比人类长远

吃饱玉米，丹顶鹤群又上路了
它们的精灵，还在田野里跳动

Wang Ping 王屏

Confession of a Ruby-Throat

in China, xiao xin/小心 is for caution
the heart gets smaller with each step of
hesitation, the shell of xin shrunken with fear
小心—a shriveled heart spilling blood
xiao xin—blue whale's car-sized heart
pumping 10 tons of blood
through its 200-ton body

yet the heart champion belongs to us
beating 1200 per minute in our chest
a body lighter than ten pinto beans
wings and tail screeching with joy
as we dive for our beloved
neon feathers lighting the air
there's no other way to love

be careful, cries the mother
to her child tumbling forward
pulling ropes tied to his waist
xiao xin: to become small
and smaller with each step

how does a fledgling enter the sky with a fearful heart?
how do we fly without tumbling first, head to the earth?
the monster rumbles in lower fields, his lava
breaths melting hesitant feet along the path

how do we live without knowing the taste of dying
each night, our heart slows to a halt
our being, lighter than a penny, half filled with sugar

心中的河流 THE RIVER WITHIN

the other half offered to the night's lord
oh, how can we have regrets: to die each night
for tomorrow's feast, an orgy of flight and nectar—

there's no other way to live, even if
it means forever on the edge of starving
to dive into 1500 flowers daily, to cross the Gulf
with a day's food, to be alive breathlessly
wings beating 200 a second, heart firing
600 a minute at rest, and doubling for a flight—

there's no other way to cross
from Mexico to Alaska, our 2-gram body
full with nectar, the rest is our heart—enormous
thrown into the wind, into the unknown

xiao xin—courage is not an absence of fear
the secret lies in our willingness to live
hours away from death, each night
in torpor, losing half of our being
to fall out of the sky

as we fly across seas and deserts
uttering cries half human half beast

Wang Ping 王屏

红玉喉北蜂鸟的自白

蓝鲸的心脏，大如轿车
每天抽送十吨的血
而心的冠军，却属于我们
轻如芸豆的身体
娇小的心，每分跳动1200节拍
俯冲大地，灿烂的尾羽
把天空染成霓红翠绿
我们的翅膀，吹响爱情的笛哨

这就是我们活着的方式
以心跳表现生命
以生命换取爱情

夜晚降临，我们的心
停止跳动
拇指甲大的躯体
一半留给阳光
一半献给黑暗
为了花心里的盛宴
还有飞翔的狂欢
我们愿意 每晚死去 复活

尼采看见汉字"小心"
以为同等心小——每一步犹豫
心就小了一圈
小心，妈妈边喊边拉起绳索
——拽回学习走路的孩子
小心：每迈一步，世界便走得更小

地心里，黑暗轰鸣

心中的河流 THE RIVER WITHIN

呼吸的岩浆，融化每一步的迟疑
充满胆怯的心，如何送雏鸟飞入篮天？
我们又如何倒栽着，出入人间，品尝生死？

这就是我们唯一活着的方式
每天采集1500口花蜜
每晚睡在生死的边缘
我们的心多么微小
安静时，每秒十拍
飞翔中，迅增一千
我们的念想多么巨大
0.8两的身体
一半载心，一半载蜜
带上一天的口粮
穿越墨西哥湾
飞向阿拉斯加

就这样，我们屏息活着
把心头的点点滴滴，全部甩进风里
甩进未知——
这是我们唯一的飞翔方式

勇气，也许不是胆怯的敌人
却是永生的秘密：

我们愿意　世世代代
夹在光明与黑暗的瞬间
承担天堂与人间的信使

我们选择　年年月月

59

Wang Ping 王屏

走进死亡
以全部的生命
换取俯仰天地的自由

每时每刻，我们准备
轻装穿越宇宙
吹着半人半鸟的口哨

注：
尼采看到汉字的"小心"，以为中国文化太过拘谨。我有感写下此诗。中国文化确实有小心的一面，但更有红玉喉北蜂鸟探索星辰大海的巨心。

红玉喉北蜂鸟是北美最小、最美、最让人惊奇的候鸟，也是心脏的冠军。它每天必须采集大量的花蜜来维持生命，到了晚上，必须进入假死，以维持生命所需的最低能量。通常活不到一年，但一年后不死，就能活6-8年。此鸟是印第安阿滋太克族太阳神的象征，代表战争、和平、永恒、美。其羽毛是阿滋太克武士的必佩品。

心中的河流 THE RIVER WITHIN

Sky 天 Earth 地 Human 人

It's April and snow
Falls; falling on highland's trees
Snow—fallen—it's blood

Sisterhood

We speak through the cranes
Our spirits move with the wind
Behind clouds—a moon

What Keeps Us Going

The hand that touches
Daily, the stillness within
Rain, face of spring ghost

Crane Memory

Our breasts hold it all
Lands of stories, shores of time
Rivers, fields, old nests

天地人

Each morning the sun
Hearts clear, renewed. Each night
Dreams—sail a blue sea
In between—sentient beings
Cradled by heaven and earth

Wang Ping 王屏

Sky Earth Human

At twilight, in the blind, things near become distant. Things distant become close. The birds, flying in large flocks, bring sky to earth, bring fields to rivers, bring south to north, east to west, bring memory to us, bring us to the beginning of sky and earth. The twilight, at the fork of day and night, opens to an invisible world, and the birds are our guides, if we allow it, along with salmon, sturgeons, cycads, gingkoes, dawn redwoods, glaciers…

As the world becomes crowded with desire, we become nomads, wandering from place to place, seeking a better life. How do we carry our ancestral spirits in our breasts? How do we carry home in our limbs, spines, souls?

The cranes know wind, and the instincts for flight. We have poetry—words with wings.

四月

是残暴的月
风暴压住平原
雪——堆积——如血

姐妹

我们与丹顶鹤结伴
我们的精魂随风而行
乌云后面,盈满的四月

推动我们的手

无影无踪,却每时每刻
不肯死去的心——平稳前进
春天在雨中做鬼脸

丹顶鹤的记忆

我们的胸装满大地的故事
我们的翅膀见证大海的潮汐
还有迁徙的河流、田野、鸟巢

天地人

每天,升起的太阳
洗涤我们的心灵。每晚
我们的梦,驶入深蓝
天地间——芸芸众生
被爱还是被弃,皆与一念

Wang Ping 王屏

黎明前的黑暗，把周围的一切推向遥远，把遥远拉回身边。天空里，成千上万的丹顶鹤从墨西哥飞往西伯利亚。 它们让天亲近大地，让河流开垦田野，让南方柔软北方，让东风滋润西风，让记忆描绘我们的脑海，让我们回到开天辟地的原始。徘徊在岔路口的黎明，打开了无形无状的世界。如果我们愿意，丹顶鹤可以为我们带路，还有鲑鱼，中华鲟，铁树，银果，红杉，冰川。
欲望把人间塞的拥挤不堪，我们漂流，寻找新家，心中装满先辈，脊梁顶着老家。
丹顶鹤知道风的走向，知道如何借力飞翔。我们知道诗歌——让每个字插上翅膀。

Skin Deep

Do you know how elephant skin
Cracks like dried earth, how much water
Held in its troughs and ridges, running
Like streams and rivers through her delta?
Do you know her skin is the largest and
Most sensitive organ for bonding
Her beauty, skin deep, aging with grace?
Do you know how she' loved by her children
The map keeper for land, water, food, graveyard?
Do you know her neurons—
Ten times more than our brain
Her hippocampus large enough to hold
Every story, love, pain, sorrow?

Can you hear her silent calls
Traveling ten kilometers underground
Her infrasound inaudible to our ears?
But if we listen, we can feel
Her forehead vibrating with love

If we learn how to treasure—
Our kin, our Grandma
Keystone of Africa
Skin of the earth

Wang Ping 王屏

渗透皮肤

你可知大象的皮肤也会像土地一样龟裂?
你可知它的皱褶包含多少水——
如小溪河流沿着身体的河谷流淌?
你可知她的皮肤是最大最敏感的亲情器官?
你可知她的美,渗透皮肤?
并随着年龄不断增长?
你可知她如何受到晚辈的珍爱?
不仅仅是因为她持有土地,水源,食物与墓地的地图。
你可知她的神经元大我们十倍?
她的记忆中心可保存
每一个故事,每一次的爱情,伤害与悲伤?

你可听到她那无声的呼喊?
在地下以每小时十公里的速度奔跑?
她的次声波虽然无法抵达我们的耳膜
但如果你用心倾听,你可以感觉到
爱时刻在她的额头震动

假如你听得到
那你就知道
如何珍爱我们的祖先
我们的祖母
非洲的基石
地球的皮肤

The Language of Cephalopod

She doesn't have a bone, but her whole body is integrity.
She has eight arms, three hearts, her blood is blue with faith
and a solid plan. Her cephalo is her pods, her limbs are
her heads, and she has millions of cells to display her
intentions
in the manner of fireworks. She wears thoughts on her skin,
traveling from red to purple to blue to white to dark
at God's speed. She opens jars, steals crabs from lab tanks
and frees herself into the sea through sewage.

She's the master of disguise and escape artist,
wearing her dreams up in her bumpy sleeves,
spreading her intelligence through her arms.
She's a loner, but when she loves, it's a beak
to beak, 8-armed embrace. After mating,
she lays eggs, watches her babies hatch, then dies.

She sheds her shells in exchange for freedom,
at the cost of life, but no matter. Young like a newborn,
older than dinosaurs, she's freer than a bird and
smarter than a whip. Her whole being has evolved
as thought, word, syntax—
Displayed from skin to skin.

What you see is what you feel.
What you feel is what you see.
A circuit of intent, expression and goal.
A cycle of telepathy, passion and grace.

Wang Ping 王屏

Chameleon of thought.
Plume of the sea.
She is our enigma of Kabbalah,
Dao Dejing, Heart Sutra.
Her ten thousand eyes in eight hands
hold our non-sense of
time and space
cause and effect
beginning and end …

She's our Bodhisattva
Goddess of language
Writing mercy and love
In her pure black ink
Across our continent of mind

头足纲的语言

她没有一根骨头，却从头到脚都是铁骨铮铮
她有八条胳膊，三颗心，血管淌着全是蓝色的信念
她的头是足， 她的肢体是头
数百万的细胞同时开放，以烟花的形式
表达意念。她的心思布满全身
姹紫嫣红，瞬息万变
她会开瓶盖，从水缸里偷螃蟹
从下水道溜出，去看看大海
她是伪装大师，逃脱艺术家
疙疙瘩瘩的胳膊上闪耀着她的梦想

心中的河流 THE RIVER WITHIN

她有多重的智商，条条通往手心
她喜爱孤独，但她爱的时候
是八条手臂的拥抱。产卵后
她日夜守护，直到所有的孩子出生
才会悄然离世。每次换壳
都有死亡陪伴，但为了自由
她在所不惜。她年轻得如同婴儿
她年长，长过恐龙
她比鸟儿自由，比鞭子犀利。
她的生命，随着思想，词语，语法—
沿着皮肤，一层层演化、展现
你看到的就是你感觉到的
意图与目的—同时表达
激情和优美—同体展现
思想的变色龙
海洋的花朵
你是卡巴拉的生命之树
道德经和心经的公案
你的手和千眼
握着解开时空、因果的密码
她是我们的观音
她是语言的女神
用漆黑的墨水
把爱和慈悲
泼满我们意识的陆地

Wang Ping 王屏

Things That Matter Catch Us by Surprise

The air trembles with anticipation
Somewhere nearby and faraway
A miracle lingers
Deep in the northern woods
A wolf courts Red Riding Hood
A man, caught by the morning news
Forgets his dog under the bush, swollen
With puppies. Somewhere in China
A little peasant girl dreams of college
As she reads hand-copied Shakespeare
Behind bags of rice, soap, pesticide, pickles

I believe every turn I've made
Is touched by an angel
Someone somewhere has guided me
Through the tangled paths
Now I stand at the confluence of two great rivers
Alone and surrounded by prayers & spirits
The air vibrates with wonders
Children are coming home
With birthday cards
And a copper house for birds

心中的河流 THE RIVER WITHIN

最不在意的事总是出其不意地追上你

空气里颤抖着某种期待
某个奇迹在远近的某个地方徘徊
北方林子的深处
大灰狼对着小红帽甜言蜜语
一只怀孕的狗在树阴里喘息
一个男人在树下读报
东海的某座小岛上
一个女孩躲在合作社农药袋后面
翻阅莎士比亚手抄本
梦想关闭了十年的大学

我们走过的每一个十字路口
都有神灵的触摸
指点我们走出荆棘之路

站在两条大河的交汇处
这里充满了精灵和祈祷
还有神奇在摇摇晃晃
孩子们快要回家了
拿着给我的生日卡
还有铜铸的鸟屋

Wang Ping 王屏

Turn Your Face to the Sun and Shadows Fall

Everything remembers something … it must

The crow remembers the hands
That trap or feed, the river
Remembers raccoons' feet in its muddy
Beach, the beach remembers willows, bones
And pebbles in cottonwood roots
The root remembers the nest and its fledglings
In the talons of memories, the child
Hears the sound of mother calling
Her name at dusk. In the twilight, a larva
Remembers the rain and wind of migration
And the black cliff remembers flowers
Hanging like ghost stars on a molten sea

A cicada bursts through the shell
—dew-drenched wings—
quivering

And one by one
In the meadow of remembrance
Forget-me-nots spread their wings
Long roots
Nailing us to the earth

The sea holds its own code to the moon
The azalea cradles its password to the spring
And the beauty, its tapestry of time
Impossible to hold, but with patience

心中的河流 THE RIVER WITHIN

We may be given a key
To a grace from within

把你的脸对准太阳

所有的事物便有了记忆

乌鸦记住那只打它或喂它的手
河流记住浣熊在河床里留下的脚印
河滩记得垂柳，鱼骨
还有卡在棉花树根里的鹅卵石
树根记得枝桠上的鸟窝，嗷嗷待哺的小鸟
记忆的爪尖，紧紧抓着
母亲吆喝我们回家吃饭的声音
黄昏,地下的幼虫想起雨点和风
乌黑的悬崖回忆着花朵
如星魂，点缀沸腾的岩浆

等待17年的红眼蝉出壳
颤抖的翅膀
沾满露水

在记忆的草坪上
勿忘我展开翅膀
一朵接着一朵
根
深深地扎进土地

Wang Ping 王屏

美—编织时间的机器
谁能挡住你的梭子?

杜鹃花含着春天的钥匙
大海冲刷月亮的密码
而灵魂只记得住
优美

What Holds

When eyes cradle a lover's curve
When bees hum in the throat of a rose

When birds feast on red-eyed cicada
Ending a seventeen-year old dream from the deep

When baby girls cry out from markets, police stations
Weeping mothers hovering in nearby woods

When leaves sway with cicada shells and nymphs burrow into the ground
Another cycle of dreams, another summer of song and birth

When my four-year-old son shouts
Mother, mother, my heart's on fire

Trees, bugs, fish
An ocean begins in a drop of rain

For ten minutes at dawn
The broad-leaf epiphyllum blooms with fury

We live, fear notwithstanding
Memory holds us to this world

Wang Ping 王屏

是什么让我们飞翔

当双眼抚摸爱人的曲线
蜜蜂在玫瑰的深处哼鸣

当群鸟饱餐出土的红眼蝉
瞬间了却等候17年的美梦

当幼虫入土,挂满蝉壳的叶子摇晃
新一轮的生命展开又一场夏日歌声

当我四岁的孩子脱口喊出
妈妈,妈妈,我的心在燃烧

当树木、昆虫、栖鸟、飞鱼
当一滴雨,启动大海的心脏

当昙花在黎明悄悄展开
惊世的仙掌,无声无息

人间是多么艰辛,而记忆
让我们飞翔,落地,生根

心中的河流 THE RIVER WITHIN

The Story of Stones

You beckon me to follow
Into the shallow bed

Two children play at the river's source
A pebble drifts through clouds of gas

It's been a long dry fall
The river bed parched for a snowstorm

Marbles, granite, pink alabaster
Each speaking a Babylon tongue

Magma cools into rocks, sand, soil
Fens, rains, wind, roots flowing like currents

So thin is the stone's inner wall
So narrow is the path to love

You rub the green chert with saliva
Releasing ghosts from its oxidized face

The way we repeat ourselves
Hanging like trees on ocean's cliff

Stones under the weight of the sea
We sing into the wind, pockets heavy with gifts

That feel of a stone in hand … that smell … that taste … that color and shape of groundmass polished to a section … that accumulation of strata sleeping under forests … sculpted by

Wang Ping 王屏

splashing ... that breathing of minerals ... that order of the universe ... that wonder ... that awe ... that light of the last autumn day ... that wet breath—impossible to say in words ... all said in a stone

石头的故事

你牵住我的手
走进干旱的河床

两个孩子在河的源头嬉戏
满满的鹅卵石,飘过大气层的云彩

这是个冗长的旱秋
干裂的河床,渴望暴风雪的到来

大理石,花岗岩,粉红雪花石膏
各自讲述自己的巴比伦

曾是炙热的岩浆,让岁月碾为沙土
沼泽里,雨风裹着草根呼吸

岩石里的缝隙是多么狭窄
通往世间的路是多么崎岖

你蘸着口水摩擦绿燧石
打开氧化的脸,释放鬼神

心中的河流 THE RIVER WITHIN

挂在海边悬崖的树上
我们不断地重复自己

被压在海底的石头
沉重的礼物,装满我们的手

那种把石头握在掌心的感觉　　　那沉淀几亿年石基的颜色和形状　　　那在树林下沉睡的地层　　　那被浪花雕塑的海岸
矿石的呼吸　　　宇宙的秩序　　　那种气味　　　那种神奇与惊叹　　　那秋日最后的天光　　　那任何语言都无法表达的故事
全部由石头述说

Wang Ping 王屏

Jewelweed

At sunrise, I row. This morning the river is choppy. Behind me in the bow seat, Master K is silent. I feel his patience. My body is slow, slowing down to the change of the season, a dam of dampness and heat building to shore against the oncoming of a cold front.

I'll give myself needles tonight, I tell myself, to dredge the damp and alleviate the stagnation along the liver and gallbladder meridians.

Master K has a grand piano in his grand living room that makes its own music when a key is played. He bought it after his wife left with their two children. When snow falls on the Mississippi, he goes to Thailand, helping women to repair houses, fight off men. When the river thaws, he comes home to row and carve. Master K is also a master carpenter. He eats raw vegetables only, for thirty years.

The river heaves. Our boat cuts the waves …

Along the riverbank, jewelweeds stand next to stinging nettles and poison ivy, an antidote for the burnt skin. Their translucent stems look like human bones and joints. Plants resembling human organs will heal those organs, I learned from my herb master, like strawberries for the heart inflammations, pears for cooling the lungs, and avocados to warm and moisten the uterus. Will the jewelweeds ease the pain in joints, and connect a torn tendon or ligament?

Master K sprinkles a seed into my palm. It's tiny, a period at the end of a sentence.

"Touch it, gently, with your fingertip," he says.

It explodes in the center of my palm and flies off.

"The seed contains so much energy. Just a touch, and it takes off."

We come out of the water drenched with the river.

"How did I do this morning, Master?

"You didn't do worse," says Master K, smiling.

Later I learned that the seed is called touch-me-not. It soothes inflamed hearts and heals scattered spirits. My friend told me it's called *Makahiya* in Filipino: the shy one, the reticent one, their nerve endings open to the slightest suggestion.

Wang Ping 王屏

珠草

天还没亮，我就去密西西比河训练划艇。今天有西南风，河水波浪起伏。后座的K大师一言不发，整条河，只有我们的浆声。

我的身体沉重，像是灌满了水。秋天换季，体内开始积累湿气，来对付即将来临的寒流。

今晚得给自己扎针，打通肝经和胆经，排除湿气，活血化瘀。

K大师家里有一架大钢琴，音质极优，每一个琴键发出的声音，让人浮想联翩。那是他的前妻带着孩子离开后，他为自己买的。每年第一场雪降临明州，他就背着背包，里面装满坚果，去泰国过冬，帮那儿的女人修房子，和欺负她们的流氓打架。河水一解冻，他就赶回家，划艇，种菜，做木工挣钱。

K大师吃了40年的素，连鸡蛋牛奶都不碰。

河水起伏，我们的船在浪里穿行。

河岸上，珠草亭亭玉立，站在刺寻麻和毒漆藤之间。那些让人闻风丧胆的毒汁，可用珠草做解药。半透明的节梗，粗壮有力，如同人骨与关节。当地的草药师曾告诉我：植物长的像哪个器官，就能滋润修复那个部位，比如草莓可以消除心火，梨子润肺，牛油果滋养子宫。

那珠草是否能修补我摔裂的膝盖骨？

K大师捏了一点种籽，撒在我的手心。黑色的种子，点点滴滴，似乎要为我们的故事点上句号。

"轻轻地碰，用你的指尖。"

句号在我的手心里爆炸，飞走,带走未曾说完的故事。

"这些种子含有巨大的能量，一触即爆。"

我们上岸后，全身被浪花打得湿透。

"大师，我今天划得如何？"

"不比上次差吧，" 他微笑着说。

我笑了，那是大师最高的评语。

回家后，我查了查珠草的来历，又名"别碰我，" 北美土著人用来消除心火，安抚惊恐失散的魂魄。我的女友告诉我，菲律宾人把这种植物称为 "玛咖西亚"——害羞的人，沉默寡言的人，其神经末梢对外界极其敏感，就像大自然的诗人和艺术家。

Part II
Food for Gods

Food for Gods

Do you know fungi? Have you tasted their flesh?
Do you know what you see is their flower, what you eat is their
    genital?
Feel their body mass under your feet, running like rivers & fires.
Marvel at the oldest life on earth, the tallest, fastest and
    wildest thing,
Alive in our nose, mouth, throat, intestines, anus, soil, water,
    air, lava?
Who'd know, of every plant on earth, there are ten more
    fungal species,
500,000 fungal spores in our pillow, 7 trillions in a puffball?
See its mycelium web, spreading several miles, in a thimbleful of
    soil,
Holding 90% weight of a forest? Do you know a forest
Can live without birds or us, but starves without fungi?
They eat dead trees & rocks, turning debris, plastic, Styrofoam
    into food.
Imagine the earth without fungi, crushed under debris,
    drowning in toxins!
Test their strength, watch how a Shaggy Mane lifts 400 kg
    asphalt,
Transforming the basalt globe into a green earth, together
With virus and bacteria? Oh hear them sing, moan, dance
In our guts, telling us what to eat, how to feel.
Please feel their pulse, slow, fast, up, down, leveling bread,
Brewing beer, wine, making medicine, dropping LSD, lifting us
    to gods.
Watch them dance in clusters, on trees, under moonlight.
Bring them to your nose, inhaling their fragrance of five elements.
Are you yet in awe, watching them rise from fires, floods, storms,

Wang Ping 王屏

Plagues and wars like warriors, artists, singers, scientists,
    Daoists!
216 species of them, hallucinogenic, humming as messengers
Between gods and earthlings, as dark taxa?
Have you seen their mapped DNA—only one molecule away
    from us?
For thousands of years, Chinese named them 灵芝
Reishi—magic shrooms for healing and love, for immortality!
Yes, they are foods from gods, for gods, key to other dimensions.
They are us, our body as a kingdom of fungi, virus, bacteria
A forest of symbiont of wonders and magic.
So be fungi! Be humans! Be gods!
Transformers of elements, artists on earth, poets of life.

Ode to Virus

Our cell is a hundred times bigger
Our body? Ten million larger!
But why are we so terrified of you
Quantum buggers on earth?
You're so puny, 50 millions of you in a teaspoon
of water, and 500 millions on a pinpoint

Is it because you outnumber all life together
On earth, ten million more than all the stars in space?
Because you live on the edge of life
As a hijacker, parasite, cuckoo, vine
Clinging, copying, sucking life out of your hosts
Turning us into your slaves, zombies, mutants?

Or because life is impossible without you:
No bacteria, cells or trees, no brains or civilization?
Because 8 % of you are buried deep in our genomes
As provirus, as our core makeups of DNA
Jumpstarting our T cells to fend off invaders?
When we get sick, it means you, provirus
Is dozing off, taking a break?

Because you spread like metaphors, defying space, time and logic
Quantum leaps from bacteria to bacteria, mosquito to mosquito
Through saliva, tears, sweat, mucus, blood, skin
Bird to bird, bat to bat, human to human?
Or a tossup between bat to bird, bird to swine, swine to human …
As flu, polio, small pox, herpes, AIDS, Zika, rabies, Ebola,
    SARS, Covid-19 …
Turning the world into a Zombie land?

Wang Ping 王屏

Because you suck our blood and steal our cells,
Then mutate our genes into cancer
Or turn starch and fat into your food, so we get fed too?
Is that why you kill us and keep us alive at the same time
Building our immunity, then making us ill so we get stronger?
Are you biological pumps to jolt life, accelerate decay?
Without you, we'd be buried under debris, bodies, woods?

So quantum buggers from cosmos?
Should I hate you or love you or both?
I want to expel you but I need you to live
I need to kill you, but killing you also kills me
because I'm part of you! You're Vampire of the Earth!
The most terrifying, most beautiful in your crowns
With your efficiency, guile, intelligence!

Ultra vires, power beyond law and logic
You are not alive, yet live everywhere!
You're our enigma, our karma
You're the poison we have to live with and can't live without
In fact poison is your Latin name
Chinese made it even worse: bingdu—病毒—diseased virus

Is that why you gave us Spanish Flu, SARS, Swine, Bird?
Or you're just being you, a trickster, a teacher and master
Showing us how to respect all sentient being on the planet
Including you, Corona; the only way to handle you
Is to embrace you, the way we keep our enemy close
Building up our pro-viruses so that bad ones can't occupy?

心中的河流 THE RIVER WITHIN

Is immunity nothing but billions of you negotiating
Space in our body, on the planet? Is this another word for
Balance, equilibrium, co-habitat?
Is this your equation of Life=Love2?

Wang Ping 王屏

Where the Yangtze Stands behind the Three Gorges Dam

From naked mountains, crows cry and cry
Monkeys throw corns and rocks at cruise boats

No more sandaled porters trekking along the cliff
No more temple bells sailing us into a whirling night

2 million displaced hearts, 50 million feet of broken
Intestines, every inch mangled under a man-made lake

Where is our Goddess of Rains and Clouds?
Only gibbon ghosts wailing behind a clogged dam

Notes:
1. Broken intestines:
   In 400 AD, Duke Heng entered the Three Gorges with his troops. One of his soldiers caught a baby monkey. The mother followed the fleet for hundreds of miles, until she finally jumped on the ship to reunite with her baby. She dropped dead as soon as she held her child. The duke ordered an autopsy, and saw that every inch of the monkey's intestine was broken from sorrow. Furious, he ordered the soldier to be punished by facial tattoos. Since then, "broken intestines" became a metaphor for extreme sorrows and trauma.
2. Goddess of Rains and Clouds
   In the legend of the Three Gorges, the Goddess of Rains and Clouds is the symbol of love and fecundity.

心中的河流 THE RIVER WITHIN

Everest—After Passing Three Checkpoints without a Permit

Heat waves from the end of August, no rowing at daybreak
Children asleep in their rooms, I'm alone with the world

Sounds of prayer flags, eyes on Mount Everest
Behind me, watching soldiers, machine guns in hands

A Chinese without ID or permit—mermaid of the earth
One leg in Old Man River, the other in the Yangtze

Keep walking, said the guide, don't run or look back
The most dangerous place can be your safest haven

Behind dams, fishermen catch trash from the darkened Yangtze
My bleeding feet open a path between the West and East

The sun comes out of the monsoon's rain and mist
Everest offers its splendor for the brave hearts

2000 laughing angels blindfold the soldiers' eyes
2000 flags from the Mississippi fly over the snowcaps

My bank is empty of cash, but my dream full with fruit
I've pledged my remaining years to rivers and mountains

Wang Ping 王屏

October Snow: for Amy from Georgia

I remember snow: wet snow, dry snow, icy snow, blizzard snow, whiteout snow, snow storm, snow that buries houses and animals alive, snow that drives deer, turkey and foxes out of the woods and eat my red cedars clean …

But this first snow in October is special: earlier than expected, gentle and firm in its falling from heaven, a virgin mother to her infant earth: look at me, embrace me, enjoy me, and you'll be loved, immensely.

I remember Amy's face, so beautiful and vivid, crumbled under the weight of the word snow.

"I can only sit by the fireplace, wrapped up, and crochet, during the 5 months of snow."
We laugh, our bellies full with salmon, shrimp, curry, turkey and Chinese broccoli, food from my garden, farmer's market, sea and land, food from the compost in the cycle of seasons, sun, rain, snow.

"Please love snow," we say, "triplet of H_2O, true magic of nature. It can do things her sisters of water and gas can't even imagine, like carrying your weight for ski, skate, snow-mobile, snow-angel, like wiping out bugs and diseases, draping the world with a bridal veil.

But do it slowly, beautiful Amy from Georgia. Let your cells open to the winter magic, frost by frost, flake by flake, snow by snow. No need to wrap yourself in down coat when the first snowflake falls. The ground is still simmering with summer's

心中的河流 THE RIVER WITHIN

heat, throbbing with life from fungi, bacteria, bugs, worms, roots ... feel the fire with your soles, pull the heat to your heart that pumps blood to your limbs, kidneys, livers, stomach, heart, lungs, brain ... until you become one with the ground, the air, the snow—Minnesota's wonder, until you rejoice at the sight of the first flake, her first touch on your rosy cheek, until you glide along the Mississippi River Gorge, the crown jewel of the 4th longest river on earth, through the ancient trees and bogs of the Crosby Farm, Hidden Falls, the walking Minnehaha ... its small laughter, each breath in and out of our lungs, each pulse through our veins, each thought from our mind, each heartbeat in sync with the first snow falling on us.

Until we love snow like Eskimos, Tibetans, yaks, moose, leopard, bears, trees ...

Wang Ping 王屏

Fox

All night long I'm the fox spirt
Breathing through the fog of sulfur

A forest in your desert sea
A fossil heart bound to my chest

Taiji along the smoking ring
Limbs rise and fall with heaving Pele

Liquid rocks flow towards the sea
Rivers of fire through parched fields

Rain of molten love
The river has opened my rib cage

The Way is open. Are we ready to cross
Fox spirits from the Ring of Fire?

心中的河流 THE RIVER WITHIN

Highway 61

> *Oh, God said to Abraham, "Kill me a son"*
> —Bob Dylan

There is a snake on the Mississippi Blvd
Coiling on asphalt, tiny tongue flicking, flickering
Patterns of black, white and green, young, vibrant
I'm supposed to fear this thing, its poison, its snaky nature
But its eyes brimming with so much life…I smile
Pull out my phone to capture this wonder out of entropy.
A biker comes towards us, his bike armed with boulder
Tires, coming at us like a train. He has a bike path
Designated just for him, but he prefers our path
He knows his "rights." He claims them the way
Settlers claimed Turtle Island on horseback
On your right, move, he shouts!
So I dash out of his way, his $2000 bike & 200-lb. flesh
Rolling over the snake, the perfect circle she just made
With her young body, now severed into pieces
Connected only with her snake skin
The circle is broken, her life broken …
I'm not supposed to cry, to pity a sneaky snake
But my heart weeps for the young innocence
So vital, so snakelike, just a second ago
I could have protected her by standing my ground
I could have shouted at the biker to shove his butt
To the bike path. But what's a snake, killed in millions
Their venom extracted to make drug for our blood pressure?
I'm not supposed to cry, not supposed to
Feel for some stupid snakes or horseshoe crabs
Their ancient blue blood drained in cages for Covid-cure.
But isn't a life a life is life, no matter

Wang Ping 王屏

What form it takes, snake or crab or mouse?
A second ago, she was coiling in a cosmic circle
Desiring nothing but a speck of space on earth
Learning how to catch her first bug
A second later, she is a shell
A splash of wet green on an asphalt road
That runs along the Mississippi from Itasca to the Gulf
This Great River Road, reserved for humanity only
This Highway 61, made immortal by Bob Dylan's voice
Oh, God said to Abraham, "Kill me a snake."

Crab and Catfish

In the river, they live apart
For food and respect
In Chinatown, they're stacked in crates
Waiting to be steamed or fried
Until a hung-over worker spills their worlds

The catfish slither and slide
Gasping belly dance on the concrete
The crabs move sideways
Crushed pincers raised
As if they own the world
The sidewalk becomes a carnival—
Prancing shoppers dodge the slimy danger
Laughing kids kick and stamp
The owner swears at the top of his lungs

A city where killing takes place daily
Like the moon circles the earth
And trees fall for highways and cows
No reason to cry for the bottom feeders
Or for the little girl in a dingy bakery
Devouring her noodles and wanting more
Soy sauce gleaming at her mouth in catfish whiskers

And here they come
The ginger-colored young
One eye hanging on the cheek like a rosary bead
On its back rides the baby crab
Legs all gone except for the pincers
Crushed shell glowing with breathing gills

Wang Ping 王屏

In the water, they hate each other's guts
Now like the mandate of heaven and earth
They charge through the human wall
Toward Canal Street—where
Home awaits, in their belief

The crowd parts like water
The city halts—watching the lowest of the low
Plunge into the sea of traffic
Behind them—a bloody trail of faith

I cry out, alone in the crowd
Homesick for my archipelago
In the East China Sea

心中的河流 THE RIVER WITHIN

Donald Judd's Secret Paradise in Marfa

The roof is gone
The ground crumbles under
Grass on concrete
A bird folds its origami wings
In the aluminum box

House of mirrors
This shadow world
Is it less
Than what eyes can see?

To see is to believe
Or blind?
Across the desert sea
A mirage of mirage
In the mirror of twilight

Time bursts in all directions
The wall will soon crumble
The wall is crumbling soon
The wall crumbles
A dream within a dream
In the sea of illusion

Wang Ping 王屏

The Instinct to Swarm

That allows us to make decisions:
What to order for lunch, or basic perceptions—
Signals flooding from the eyes or hearts,
Struggling for balance, juggling
Between time and space, two houses
Across the river of stars. Eye of the hail—
The small chime turns in the cloud, its copper heart
Swinging left to right, right to left.
The old lawn mower roars with fresh gas.
And the grass, smelling like hay rolling into the sea
Brings tears to the eyes. "She weeps when she thinks of
Her lover at sunset," her son confirms.
How does a heart heal? The answer may lie
In the inner swarm, tangled, running ahead of time.
How does our brain see what we see?
Or feel? How do we not run from pain, but stand
Face to face? It's been four months since April,
The cruelest of all. The trees are still green
And birds still singing, but the grass is littered
With thorny shells of acorns, biting hands and feet
As I dig weeds on my knees with a steak knife.
Every day, I must learn how to live again.
Breathe between knocking woodpeckers and
Bleeding twilight. Hands under thighs.
I wish you only goodness and safety.
I wish all sentient beings good and safe—is
My prayer for you, for us. Our bodies apart,
But the minds still twine, with hearts as a metronome,
ticking ¾ time. I have taken off my watch long ago,
and the seat belt. Our hammock hangs between

心中的河流 The River Within

The mesh of rope and met of lights,
Flickering from the far north

Wang Ping 王屏

Oracle

In the dungeon, the rooster,
headless, crows from its chest

What's the longest journey? asked Raul
from Cuba. *There is no return after this point*

The only betrayal comes from within
The Sphinx lays down her paws in the blaze

Words open old wounds. I thought
I knew: it takes years for a scar to recede

The journey seems impossible
Then improbable, then inevitable

But for now we breathe
One miracle at a time

心中的河流 THE RIVER WITHIN

The Meridian Gate

On my father's grave
A shaggy mane lifts her skirt
A noonday demon is born
From yesterday's love

Needle between the 4th ribs
Tan zhong
The upper ocean of breath
Between breasts

Children of the moon
Roots tangled in the other world
I've wrestled with a lion
Now I marvel at mustard seeds

Bean fingers curling into the sun
Needle at *Bai Hui*
One Hundred Confluences
At the apex of scalp

The mind spins a fountain of fire
From Buddha's tear, a White Tara
If we fold our wings and listen
We may taste the honey in our bread

From asphalt, a fiddlehead
Opens its green fist
A swirling path to the moon
A pearl in the hollow of grief

Wang Ping 王屏

Breathe in *dan tian*
Thunder from Good Earth
A bridge to forgive—
Forgiven

When night comes, we go to the woods
And listen to the sounds of stars
Traveling 200 billion light years
To touch us

Eudemonia

He said something about buying more land
That would never cheat, spoil or bankrupt.
She pulled her lips down.
"More land? Oh shush, Old Man!
I got too much on my mind
In this awful place that stinks of death!"
He snorted. "But land will help you
Get some weight off your neck, my dear!"

And so back and forth till I burst out
Laughing at this bickering couple
The man turned, laughing with me.
"I'm a farmer. What about you?" he asked.
"Three years on an island in the East China Sea.
We planted rice, wheat, yams, trees, vegetables …
Now I grow flowers in my garden."

"Yeah, I love flowers," the wife chirped in.
"Corn is evil. It messes me up after I shovel
35 bushels. See my hands?"
She lifted her rheumatoid fingers.
"My neck is killing me, too.
Can we go home, dear?
I don't care for MRIs or CT scans.
They give me the creeps, make my heart flutter."

"Oh shush," said the farmer.
"Flowers are nothing but ugly weeds.
I spray when I see them in my fields."
He spat and made a sound of spraying: *pssssss*.

Wang Ping 王屏

"Soy and corn, now that's something
To behold from my combine
Emerald green in spring, golden brown in autumn
Reaching all the way into a purple horizon
Returning with pots of gold, always.
God bless, what flower on earth can beat that beauty!"

"Oh, you foolish old man!" hissed the wife
As she stormed off to the bathroom.

He winked at me. "Isn't she lovely?
This is our second marriage:
First time 18 years, divorced 18 years.
Why? I fell in love and married another woman.
Boy, the scandal we caused in Plato,
Town of 97 households, 320 people.
It was a tornado blasting through.
Well, what is love if not a tornado?
I feared she might not survive, but she stood,
Lived alone in our farmhouse for 18 years.
People say she couldn't find another man
Where everyone is married and those still single
Are no good—damaged goods.
But I know better. She never stopped loving me.
After my open-heart surgery, I lost everything:
Wife, land, farm, cattle, money …
She invited me to dinner, roast beef and potatoes.
Boy, I cried and laughed over my plate
Chewing the delicious meal I could only smell in dreams
A week later, we married each other again, for real.

心中的河流 THE RIVER WITHIN

That was 16 years ago. How old am I?
Want to guess? 60? Nah! I'm 80.
Oh, thank you! I'm happy as a lark
As long as I can climb my combine
To plough into the soil.
I was born to be a farmer.
I'll live and die as a farmer."

The wife came back, smile on her face
As she sat down and held his hand.
He said something to her ear.
She pulled down her lips, slapped
His wrist and they laughed.

I laughed with them, the farmer and his wife
Who may not know about Plato or Aristotle
Or his *eudemonia*, but they thrive
Despite his affair and open-heart surgery,
Despite their divorce and second marriage,
Despite waiting at DCI with a fluttering
Heart and rheumatoid hands
Who live and die as a farmer and farmer's wife
In tiny rural Plato, Minnesota.

This is their *eudemonia*—
To love the land, love life, love each other.

Wang Ping 王屏

Jewel of the Himalaya

It's not the gemstones or fossils
Sold to tourists and museums,
Says Sherpa Lhamu of Dingboche.
It's not even Dalh Baht, the lentil soup
Keeping us nimble like mountain goats.

The West calls it potato.
Chinese call it tudou 土豆 bean of earth.
We call it aloo—small, muddy, bountiful,
Heavier than our mountains.
In spring, before snow melts
The whole village stands still:
No cooking, no music, no fire or visitor.
In silence we plough, bending over the soil
Until every seed enters the earth.
Then we wait, outside the stonewalls,
No human allowed into the fields,
Only yaks and dogs to enrich the soil.
When rain comes and leaves push through ice,
We crawl in, children and women,
Baskets and prongs in hands,
Weeding, breaking clay,
Plant by plant, field by field, mountain by mountain.

There's no other way around it,
Says Lhamu from Dingboche, standing tall,
20000 feet above the sea, on the Nepalese Plains.
Aloos need to be cradled like this,
Three times a year, on our hands and knees…
She laughs, teeth sparkling against her chapped face,

心中的河流 THE RIVER WITHIN

Purple and beautiful from the Himalaya sun.
Above us, the Amadablam looms.
Under our feet, aloos dig into thin soil and boulders,
Dissolving minerals, turning the sun into flowers—
White, lilacs petals with yellow hearts.

It's more than a muddy potato or a small bean of the earth
It's aloo, aloo, aloo…
Call her, raise her from the deep,
Jewel of the Himalaya,
Our goddess, our Mother,
Savored by her children
Of warriors and peace,
Says Sherpa Lhamu of Dingboche from Everest.

Wang Ping 王屏

This Is My Garden

It's Saturday. I get up at sunrise, make tea, make coffee, stretch, then go out for my 12k-meter row in the Mississippi. I'm a sculler. My single boat with long oars makes social distancing super easy and fun. The river is calm. The bluffs are breathtaking. Bald eagles fly over and across, guiding my spirit.

The river is my temple, my 12k-meter long prayer, daily.

Today is Memorial Day, 2020, marking summer, growth, long days, short nights, mosquitos, flies, bees, wasps and beetles, vacations, beach, sunlight, joy, crowds … But it's quiet, too quiet, almost. Church was ordered to open, but Minnesotans follow their instincts for preservation. No choir. People are morning. America is mourning. Its death is reaching 100,000; America is sick with the virus, almost 2 millions, mostly the old, the sick, the black, brown, indigenous, the meat packers, the essential workers, the "not usual folks like us," according to some congresspeople.

Dr. Fauci warned the deaths may reach 200,000, if we are not careful.

I know it'll surpass that. I tend to add a zero after the official number.
Because 2020 is the year of 明夷, the sun is buried underground, according to the Book of Oracles I-Ching.

America's wallet is empty, along with its calendar, except for the Zoom funerals and meetings.

心中的河流 THE RIVER WITHIN

Americans are already mourning the summer.

From the river, I go to the farmers' market, downtown St. Paul, to buy seedlings for my garden. It's the best market I've ever known. I grew up with many, in China, in America, in Europe. Farmers' markets are wet markets, selling fish, meat, poultry, dairy, mushrooms, bread, fruit, vegetables and seedlings. It's still early in the season. Most vendors sell rows of flowers and vegetables. This year, vegetables sell faster than flowers. Everyone is planting their own food. Our instincts tell us to prepare for a long haul. I thread my way through the masked crowd. People are smiling, behind the masks. Even the grouchy ones relax their brows. The farmers' market is a happy place. How can it not be? Food makes people happy. Flowers makes people smile.

I buy collard greens and spinach for my garden, already full with potatoes (red, yellow, purple), tomatoes (Early Girl, Purple German, heirlooms, Zesty Stars, Lemon Boy …), pole beans, snow peas, cucumbers, broccoli, chard, collard green, cauliflower, Brussel sprouts, celery, peppers (Thai, devil, ghost, jalapeno), carrot, radish, beet, garlic, onion, chive, basil, parsley, tarragon, oregano, mint, Shepherd's purse…

They all seem to have grown a few inches from the rain last night. The ground is finally warm. It's Memorial Day. It's summer!

My potatoes are already 2–3 feet tall. I thin out some leaves, so that the pull beans and cucumbers will get enough sun to climb. Once they latch on the branches I pounded in next to the seedlings, they'll climb against the wall, the window, all the way to the second floor. I'll need a ladder to pick their fruit. Meanwhile, the potatoes are storing its starch energy underground, through the green leaves above ground. Each plant will yield a box of root. From the way they're growing, I know I'll have at least 3–400 pounds of potatoes this year. I've promised my friends some, and will store the rest in the garage closet through the winter, my "root cellar."

Home-grown potatoes are the wonder of the earth. Its taste comes close to Peru's *los papas*, not quite, but close. Once you have that taste of the mother earth on your tongue, you won't be able to tolerate the pale bland globs from a supermarket.

So are the home-grown tomatoes. One bite into their juicy flesh, you have the entire sky in your mouth, its color, glamor, sugar. This year, my garden will give me hundreds of tomatoes. I'll can and make soup with them, with leeks and squash.

On my knees, I dig and mix the earth with homemade compost and peat moss, then plant each seedling in the garden. It's full, but I always find a spot for everything. Our good earth has a spot for every life, mammal, bird, fish, insect, for every tree, plant, grass.

As I put in the last collard green, I notice last night's raindrops on King Solomon's leaves, then on hostas, peonies, ferns, dogwood, Korean maple, the remaining petals of azaleas, magnolia, the sprouting Japanese hemlock, onto the potatoes, tomatoes, cauliflower, broccoli, spinach … They shimmer and roll in the light, in the breeze, cooing like newborns.

My summer calendar may be empty, but my garden is full, lush with life, despite the mourning in America.

This is how I celebrate Memorial Day, to open the summer of 2020, to prepare its long winter.

This is my garden, my study, my lab, my temple, my river, my earth, my little universe.
I hope it's yours too.

Part III
Jerusalem, Jerusalem

心中的河流 THE RIVER WITHIN

Jerusalem, Jerusalem

It's impossible to sink in the Dead Sea, almost

Slabs of stone
Reaching from tombs—
Witness to untold stories

We didn't plan this. But every morning, when the sun opened the sky with orange and blue, the boys began to climb, up the steps, through the Jaffa Gate, the empty alleys of shops, cafes, homes, through the x-ray machines and guards, jumping sliding trudging singing towards the wall, to press their tiny faces against the cold stones in the praying sea.

Adam is Jewish. He doesn't pray.

I'm a Tibetan Buddhist. Whenever Torah is carried out, my face is covered with tears, and Adam would ask: "Are you ill?"

Nobody told them to. But when the sun went down, my five and three-year-old sons would run down the mountain, singing "Moses came down from the mountain top."

In the Turkish Bazaar
Adam had so much fun
Haggling over a T-shirt that said:
"America, don't worry
Israel stands behind you"

Barb-wired hotels along the shore
Parched camps beyond a dusty horizon

Brown workers hidden in orchards, spas, bridges
Sounds of prayer from armored compounds

Over a dollar, he haggled and haggled
His face red from the drama
"Why not give him two bucks? Not enough
To buy you a cup of coffee back home."

"You don't understand business, that's why you're poor.
No haggle, no respect.
No respect, no Israel."

Today's wind moves through Mount Olive
Slicing dream after dream
Who bestows us with this legacy?
Who can tell how much is illusion?

Stradling the cannon balls at Masada
My three-year-old son wept like an old man
His tears filling the broken cistern under his feet

Nava Applebaum, what are you doing out there at the small hour in Jerusalem? A last cup of coffee with your father before your wedding? Do you know your mother is waiting to don the bridal crown on your moon face, your bridegroom counting the stars before dawn breaks? Do you hear the bomb ticking outside? Nava, you bright-eyed flower, plucked before you bear fruit.

Isabel, the olive-skinned daughter of the Turkish Bazaar,

walked us through the maze of the old town. Her brother, a six-grader, gave us oranges from his juice stand when his mom wasn't looking. He whispered his dream of getting out of the slum, of making a movie about his Portuguese father and Arab mother, his grandparents in the West Bank. *But how could you understand this unless you speak Arabic*, he mumbled, turning away.

In the sea of the deep where mud is black and water boils with the odor of rotten eggs, in the mist of sulfur magic, people converge, the sick and old, the rich and poor, white, olive, yellow and brown. They wade with patience. They wait for miracles.

Under the boiling sun of Masada
Daddy lost his patience and
The little one got his first קסָארפ on the butt

Isabel watched us in the sunset, smile receding from her brown eyes like a tide.

Jerusalem—
Where the land ends and begins, matchless
A path for the return of wailing hearts

Oy! Regret comes only after the deed
The light of the plum blossom is gone
Only a kindling flame to light her track
How easy to get tangled
In the fire of thoughts!

Wang Ping 王屏

The three-year-old boy
Couldn't stop wailing
On the fortress of Masada

Who should laugh, who should cry?
Who could keep the land, who must go?
Who should be a master, who a slave?
Who could live, who must die?

This pain—
Has no tongue
Without our tongue
How do we appease endless storms in the heart?

Standing on Father's shoulders,
Children stuffed their prayers
Into the highest crack they could reach
A dove landed on the wall, cooing through the grass

"Will she pick out our crane?" asked the little one
"Will she bring our prayer to heaven?"

For the false desire and fate
For tears turned into flame
In smoke, dip the apple in honey
Dip hatred, blood, dip hope and despair
Dip remorse hidden in the gut
The laughing cry from children's lips
For Isabel and Nava, for every soul
To resettle in the cradle of roots

心中的河流 THE RIVER WITHIN

Dip Bethlehem, dip Jerusalem
Dip bombs, tanks, checkpoints
Dip the world plowed with sorrow
In the bowl of honey

The little ones stopped each stranger
on the cobblestone of Jerusalem

"Please repeat our password:
Shalom, shalom, shalom 和平，和平，和平 …"

耶路撒冷，耶路撒冷

在死海里，你无法下沉，也无法直立，无论你如何挣扎。

一条条石板
从古墓里伸出手脚
为掩埋的故事做证

太阳还没把天空染红，孩子们就开始爬坡，穿过嘉法门，店铺、咖啡馆、住家，穿过x-光检查机，荷枪实弹的士兵。他们边跳边唱，跑向哭墙，把小脸贴住石砖。我不知道他们在祷告还是在倾听上天的秘密。没人要求他们这么做。孩子的爸爸是犹太人，但从不祷告，也不知怎么祷告。我不是犹太人，每当《摩西五经》抬出来时，我却禁不住泪流满面，他只会问：你病了吗。我们的孩子，一个五岁，一个三岁，第一次来以色列。太阳西下时，他们挥着胖呼呼的小手，唱起"摩西从山顶上走下来"，跑下山坡。

市中心的土耳其市场
前夫亚当看中一件T恤衫，一美金

Wang Ping 王屏

上面写着："美国，你不要担心
以色列在为你撑腰。"

左边是海边的豪华旅馆，墙头插满玻璃、电网
右边，一眼望去，难民营的沙漠
早晚的祷告，从全副武装的犹太教堂里传出
来自亚洲的民工，为主人摘采蔬果，按摩，修路

为了一美金，亚当和小贩吵得面红耳赤。我说你要是喜欢，就给他两美金吧，还不够你买一杯咖啡的钱呢。他严肃地回答：你不懂生意，所以穷。没有讨价还价，就没有尊重、自主，更没有以色列。

风吹过了橄榄山
留下一地的碎梦
是谁赋予我们这堆记忆？
谁愿意说，这就是幻觉？

伊莎贝儿，橄榄肤色的女孩，带我们走出迷宫似的老街。她的弟弟，趁妈妈没看见，从小摊上拿起橘子赠送我们。他悄悄地诉说他的梦想：走出贫民窟，上大学，为葡萄牙父亲和巴勒斯坦母亲拍一部爱情片。说着说着，他低下了头："你不是阿拉伯人，怎么会懂我的心？"

这里的淤泥很沉很贵，这里的水发着臭鸡蛋的味道，这里的海早已死去。

硫磺泉，升起神秘的雾。以色列的病人、老人、富人，浸泡在这奇臭的水里，等待奇迹。

心中的河流 THE RIVER WITHIN

伊莎贝儿在夕阳里瞧着我们，眼里的微笑，潮水般的褪去。

耶路撒冷
历史从这里结束、开始、又结束
心，沿着这条纠结，盘旋
花瓣上的露珠已经消失
一支烛光，投在石板路上

悔恨，你为什么永远坐在行动的后面

小儿子兴高采烈地和哥哥爬铁球炸弹山。坐在以色列著名的古炮台上，他开始哭泣，像个老人，怎么哄都停不下。烈日当头，爸爸发脾气了。三岁的儿子第一次尝到打屁股的滋味。

谁可以大笑，谁活该倒霉？
谁可以占领土地，谁背井离乡？
谁可以活下去，谁必须死亡？

这种痛
苦得没有舌头

失去舌头
我们如何平息心头的滔天大浪？

站在父亲的肩头
儿子把祈祷叠成纸鹤
塞进最高的墙缝
一只鸽子飞到墙上，咕咕叫着

"她会把我们的仙鹤吃掉吗？"小不点儿问

Wang Ping 王屏

"她会不会把我们的祈祷带入天堂？"

为了燃烧的眼泪
为了无边的欲望
为了发不出声的呜咽
为了被硝烟烤焦的因果

我们把苦菜蘸入盐水
再把苹果蘸入蜂蜜

蘸一蘸耶路撒冷
蘸一蘸悲伤绝望
蘸一蘸断肠的剧痛
蘸一蘸伯利恒
蘸一蘸鲜血、希望
蘸一蘸孩子、老人的祈求
蘸一蘸坦克、火箭炮，铁穹
蘸吧，把我们遍体鳞伤的地球
蘸进浓浓的蜜

也许，焚烧的豆萁，会突然听见兄弟在釜里哭泣
也许，也许，我们可以拉开这些盘根错节的宿怨

我的小儿张开手臂，拦住街上的行人：
请重复我们的通行令—
Shalom Shalom Shalom 和平，和平，和平！

心中的河流 THE RIVER WITHIN

注：

2002年，我和前夫亚当带着两个儿子，跟随我们学院的考古队，去以色列的戈兰高地，挖掘古罗马遗址。我们住在戈兰高地的基布兹，以色列的集體農場。挖掘的工地上，我们可以看见叙利亚。虽然当时我不知道戈兰高地的历史，站在山坡上，我已经感觉到紧张的气氛。挖掘完后，我们带着孩子沿着以色列跑了一圈，最后来到耶路撒冷。我当时的感受，和现在对巴以的看法，基本没变。回来后，我和前夫与他的家人就以巴问题发生过不少争论，直至我决定离开。分手前，我说：所有的民族都有生存的权利，都有享受和平的权利. 尤其是同宗同族的犹太和巴勒斯坦人。连孩子都懂的道理，为什么成人就不愿做？

Passover逾越节：犹太人最大的节日，庆祝他们的祖先逃离埃及，到达耶路撒冷，获得自由。节日历时七天，最后一天全家举行长达3-4个小时的晚宴，要经过许多的仪式，包括特定的食物，讲故事，回顾历史，玩游戏。其中的食物仪式里，有没有发酵的考面饼，苦菜蘸盐水，苹果蘸蜂蜜，代表逃离的艰难，代表先苦后甜。

Shalom：希伯来问候语：愿平安与你永在。

这首诗的初稿，写于2002年，为我孩子洗礼入犹太教的拉比拉斯卡斯，对此诗完全认同。

PART IV
HOW A DROPLET
BECOMES A TSUNAMI
一滴水．海啸

心中的河流 THE RIVER WITHIN

How A Droplet Becomes A Tsunami: Field Notes from Standing Rock

一滴水．海啸

This is a peace camp
No bullets are needed
No toxic fog is needed
No sonic bomb is needed
No killing drone is needed
No military police are needed
No grenades to concuss our brain
No water cannon to freeze our bone
We come here to spread love on earth
We come to keep Earth a blue clean place
We shall stand here till blizzards fall on us
We shall stand till truth blossoms & no more
Pipelines to burn our water and land into inferno
We'll stand till buffaloes & rivers run free and happy
We shall stand till the world becomes One Nation of Peace
                              Good Sky Woman

*

On December 4, 2016, I arrived at Standing Rock with 4000 veterans, to form a human shield for the Dakotas. They have been camping at the Cannon Ball River since April, enduring daily brutal attacks from DAPL militant police.

That day, Standing Rock swelled to 20,000 people, since a Dakota woman pitched the first teepee on her land to stop pipelines from crossing the Missouri.

*

The story begins with oil.

Every day the world guzzles up 80 million barrels, 25% by the USA.

Bakken in North Dakota has abundant crude, mined through fracking, to quench our thirst for oil.

Every day, crude moves from Bakken through North & South Dakota, Iowa, Illinois, where half a million barrels gather before flowing to the Gulf, East Coast, Asia, Europe.

Crude is very toxic and explosive. In 2013, a train carrying Bakken oil derailed in Lac-Mégantic, near Quebec, spilling 1.5 million barrels. The whole town was incinerated.

66 more trains have exploded since that disaster. Each explosion costs billions. So the oil industry moves 70% of its crude through pipelines. It's safer, it claims.

Every day, pipelines leak somewhere, small and big.

Enbridge Pipeline ruptured in 2010, spilled a million gallons into the Kalamazoo.

The cleanup cost a billion dollars, and never succeeded, like the *Exxon Valdez*.

That doesn't include the price tag on the life killed in water.

*

2016, DAPL reached Lake Oahe, poised to drill under the reservoir, through Standing Rock's land.

Lake Oahe is the largest dam on the Missouri, drinking water source for the Sioux.

If the pipeline leaks, it'll be deadly for the tribe and 18 million people down the river.

Over 2,000 major leaks have occurred since 1995, including the Kalamazoo and Yellow Stone.

*

Standing Rock Tribe set up the camp and sent out calls.

200 nations answered, from the U.S., South and North America, Europe, Middle East …

The camp swelled into a united nation for peace.

*

Who are the Dakota, also known as Lakota and Sioux?

The story began with the Minnesota River, 332 miles long, a.k.a. Forgotten River.

It was once the mighty Glacial River Warren, an outlet for the glacial Lake Agassiz.

It covered Minnesota, North Dakota, Canada, gouging out the Mississippi valleys.

In St. Paul, where Fort Snelling stands, the glacial river plunges 175 feet into a gorge.

The Sioux emerged as the Mdewakanton, "those born of the waters."

The Sioux Nations stretched from Minnesota to the Rocky Mountains.

Oceti Sakowin: 7 fires, 7 councils, 7 tribes, 3 Lakotas, 4 Dakotas.

Then settlers came. They wanted the land and rivers.

They "negotiated" treaties with the Sioux, "bought" Pike Island, most of south Minnesota and Wisconsin, promising annuity and peace.

Pike Island was immediately slashed from $20,000 to $2000.

By 1858, the Sioux ceded their land except for a 10-mile tract along the Minnesota River.

The Sioux now depended on white traders. The traders robbed the Sioux blind with 400% profit.

And money never arrived. Food never arrived. Clothes never arrived.

The starving Sioux gathered at the trade buildings, demanding the promised annuity.

The traders told their chief Little Crow: go eat the grass.

The translator refused to translate, knowing it'd lead to a war. The trader forced him to translate.

That year in 1862, a starving Dakota youth took an egg from the nest of a settler's homestead.

It led to war broken out between the Sioux and America armies. The uprising lasted 6 weeks.

303 men were sentenced to die. President Lincoln reduced the number to 38.

On December 26, 1862, the Sioux were hung at Mankato, MN, one by one, on single gallows.

It's the biggest mass hanging in U.S. history.

Their bodies were buried by the Minnesota River.

Doctors, including Mayo, dug them out for "medical research."

Children, women and elders were rounded up on Pike Island, under Fort Snelling.

They had no food, clothes, or medicine for the harsh winter.

Many were frozen to the ground and never woke up.

Over 300 died of cholera.

In April, 1863, the Congress revoked all the treaties and banished the Sioux from Minnesota.

They were marched out along the river, into Nebraska, South and North Dakota.

Along the way, the settlers assaulted them with boiling water, rocks, guns …

The Minnesota River was a trail of tears and blood.

Those who reached their destinations disappeared in droughts and blizzards.

Those who stayed home were hunted down for bounties. Two more men, including the rebel leader Little Crow, were hung at Fort Snelling. The massacre becomes 38+2.

Minnesota still hasn't lifted the ban.

心中的河流 THE RIVER WITHIN

*

we welcomed you with turkey, you returned with guns and
    whiskey
we offered our feathers of hope, you returned with blankets of
    smallpox
we showed you how to honor life, you hunted down our last
    wolf, eagle, buffalo
we offered treaties for peace and co-habitat, you exiled us to
    deserts, barren plains
we showed you how we love children, you jailed them in your
    whitewashing schools
we plead you to honor our Mother, you frack her with drills,
    pumps, toxic brine
we ask you to respect our ancestors, you bulldoze burial
    grounds, sacred sites
we say NO to pipelines, you sent troops, mace, drones,
    concussion grenades

so we stand up, we stand tall, and we stand together with all
    tribes
and nations from four corners of Earth in defense of water—
blue-blood for algae, grass, trees, fruits bugs, fish, birds,
    mammals
sky, rivers, mountains, valleys
free spirit from the birth of all stars
gift for all sentient beings from our Mother
it's not ours to give away
it's not yours to steal, rob, kill

                                      Good Sky Woman

*

134 years later, the Sioux awakened their Mdewakanton, "Water of the Great Spirit."

On April 1, 2016, Joy Brown pitched her first teepee on LaDonna's land, at the confluence of the Missouri and Cannon Ball.

A second came up, then a third, then a camp, then 200 nations …

*

I traveled to Standing Rock in November and December with 2000 prayer flags made along the Mississippi, Yangtze, Ganga, Amazon, Everest.

They fluttered along the Cannon Ball, four corners of the camp.

People photographed, filmed and made their own prayer flags.

They called me "Flag Woman."

At their request, I left the flags flying on the hill overlooking DAPL troops.

*

Who am I to tell this story? I'm not a Native, not a veteran, not even a U.S. citizen.

*

心中的河流 THE RIVER WITHIN

In 2008, I took my writing class to the Minnesota River for a four-day canoe trip, guided by Sioux leader Le Moines, his wife Rose, and Jon Lurie.

Le Moines started our journey at the Upper Region Sioux, near the source of the Minnesota River, the historical marker where Andrew Myrick told the starving Sioux to go "eat grass and dung."

"The translator turned pale," said Le Moines. "He knew this insult, if translated, could spark a war. But Myrick forced him to translate, word by word, to Little Crow and other chiefs."

Le Moines' voice was deep and muddy like the turbid water of the Minnesota, a river forgotten but never disappeared.

*

Not a single student had heard of the 1862 Sioux Uprising, the mass hanging, Pike Island Internment Camp, the genocide, the bloody origin of Minnesota state, the murky water that was once the Glacial River Warren that created Great Sioux Nations and the fertile land of Midwest, its valleys, cliffs, cities … now the most polluted river on Earth, sending tons of pesticides, herbicides and fertilizers down the Mississippi creating a death zone the size of Texas in the Gulf.

*

The story rustled among tall grasses as we paddled down the Forgotten River.

Wang Ping 王屏

*

If academic learning is a flower and life is a tree, the flower will never bloom unless we dig our roots into the living soil.

"The canoe trip changed us forever. We no longer see or write about America the same way again," said students.

*

I took my classes back to rivers, the Minnesota, the Mississippi, Lake Itasca, St. Croix, the Yangtze, the Ganga, Tibet, Everest, Nepal …

*

Kinship of Rivers project was born during the trips. We became kin again with rivers.

*

We are water, 75% of us, our bones, hair, organs, brain, flesh, blood.

All water moves to rivers. All rivers move into seas. All seas connect as Panthalassa.

To pollute one drop of water is to pollute all rivers, all seas.

To hurt one tribal land is to hurt all the land on the planet.

*

The Sioux know that.

"We have the answers on how to live with this Earth. We have to share that knowledge," said LaDonna Tamakawastewin Allard, a historian from Standing Rock.

*

So the first teepee on her land, the first drop of water, rippling into a tsunami.

*

The Sioux believed they came from the center of the earth, lived on the land where the River Warren, the Mississippi and Rum River came together. After a flood they went into water and lived as underwater "people." Then a whirlpool pulled them up onto the shore, as water protectors.

*

Every morning, Standing Rock gathers at the Cannon Ball for water ceremony.

Grandma Pearl blesses women with purified water and songs.

Men wait behind

*

I found Pearl's assistant and handed her two jugs of water.

Her eyes teared when I mentioned Coldwater Spring.

"That's the sacred water from our birthplace. We use it for purification," she held the jars to her chest. "Thank you for the Mdewakanton, water of great spirit."

*

Kinship of River flags fluttered above our heads, above the Cannon Ball.

They've been blessed by rivers, mountains and the Dalai Lama, now by Standing Rock Grandma.

*

In 2010, I went to Tibet, to install a banner of six artists' work on fabric, including my poem on the back of a turtle drowning in the oil-covered Gulf. I begged a fisherman to bring the flags to an island that marked the end of the Yangtze, but he said they're ugly, scary and bad luck. I had to bribe them with a thousand Yuan to accomplish the mission. I brought the other flags to Tibet. The air was thin at 5000 meters above the sea. I gasped for air as I tied the banner with millions of prayer flags. I stepped back. Our ugly flags fluttered in the sea of prayer, transformed into beauty.

*

In the thin air, I saw thousands of people making flags of poetry and art along the Yangtze, Mississippi and other rivers, to spread peace and joy, to bring all rivers together as sisters.

*

I asked the veterans why they came to Standing Rock.

To defend our water, said Joe from California.

To defend our rights. DAPL has violated the constitutional law, said Julie from Texas.

*

Pretty Rainbow welcomed us at the Eagle Butte Community Center.

She's 97, Great Grandma of the Reservation, served as a nurse during WWII.

She's the oldest vet on Standing Rock.

"I'm serving for the right mission, finally," she said, holding my hand between hers.

*

We stationed at Eagle Butte on Dec. 3, before our march to the Standing Rock frontline, to take some pressure off the crowded Oceti Sakowin Camp.

The reservation is among the poorest in the US. Children volunteer to be adopted by white families for a chance to go to college.

Jay Cook, Iron Lightning, is one of the children. He ran away from a few families until he found a good one, went to college, now works as a ranger.

"That's my grandson in the arms of Barack and Michelle," he pointed to the photos on the wall. "They came to our land and vowed to make our life better. A promise to children is sacred. We're praying to remind him of the vow."

*

We spent the night in the high school gym, minimal equipment, but clean and spacious. Eagle Butte is generous with their children.

They fed us, thousands of vets, with eggs, bacon, sausage, fruits, nuts, milk, coffee.

*

Cars and trucks lined the ditches upside down. Blizzards had already hit this unforgiving land. A new one was on its way. Standing Rock would be colder than Mars, the radio announced.

It didn't stop the world from coming to the camp.

*

This is the nature of water: the best solvent and equalizer, the best cleansing agent, the most generous, the foundation for life, including rocks, the oldest element from the big bang.

*

H_2O—two hands cradling an open heart.

*

Water feels. Water sees. Water is.

*

When we arrived at 2:00, the camp was a boiling sea: riders standing on horses' backs cheering, girls beating drums, singing and dancing on top of RVs. I grabbed a man and asked him what was happening. He laughed and laughed, choking with tears:

"The permit to cross the river is denied. Our prayer is answered."

Standing Rock is a tsunami of joy.

*

Is it a miracle?

The camp forbids weapons and violence, including self-defense, no matter what DAPL releases on them: dogs, mace, rubber bullets, grenades, water cannons, drones, strip search, dog kennels, jail …

*

It has no electricity, no running water, no internet, no oil guzzling consumption.

*

"This is all I need: land, water, sage, prayer. I've never been so happy," wept Buffalo Hair.

*

Prayer follows the law of matter, indestructible like H_2O.

*

Sometimes it goes beyond, when it syncs with God's volition.

*

That's how a droplet becomes a ripple becomes a wave becomes a tsunami.

*

In the blinding blizzard, 4000 veterans marched to the Cannon Ball Bridge, where the Sioux hold the standoff with DAPL since April 2016. Their volition is the only weapon they need.

*

Two miles away from the bridge, Wes Clark, Jr., commander of Veterans for Standing Rock, asked Lakota elder Leonard Crow Dog for forgiveness.

*

Leonard placed his hand on his head: "We do not own the land. The land owns us."

*

Tsunami—海啸—*hai xiao*—sea whistling.

*

A sound, a drop of water, a wave, a tsunami of blue revolution from the sea floor.

心中的河流 THE RIVER WITHIN

*

A transfer of energy, wave upon wave upon wave, till it finds a home.

Part V
The River in Our Blood:
A Sonnet Crown
血液的河流：十四行诗皇冠

*To my dear friend Lord Charles de Bruce
from Scotland*

Wang Ping 王屏

I

The geese are painting the sky with a V, my lord
The Mississippi laughs with its white teeth
How fast winter flees from the lowland, my lord
And how's the highland where songs forever seethe?

At the confluence, I sing of the prairie, my lord
My joy and sorrow soar with rolling spring
Its thunder half bird, half mermaid, my lord
No poppies on hills, only ghost warriors' calling

Today is *chunfeng*—we say shared spring, you equinox
Two spirits, one on phoenix wings, one on lion's seat
Across the sea, kindred spirits, my lord
Prayer through breaths, laughing children on the street

Let's open our gift, acorn of small things
Let river move us without wants or needs

心中的河流 THE RIVER WITHIN

野雁用V勾画出天空，阁下
密西西比河笑了，浅露白牙
冬天匆匆逃离北方的湿地，我的阁下
那风笛沸扬的高地,可还是冰雪交加？

我站在河流的汇合口，阁下
喜悦悲伤随着冰潮，堆叠起落
那雷声，一半候鸟，一半人鱼，我的阁下
山岗上没有罂粟，只有勇士游荡的魂魄

今天是春分，我们说共享，你们要平分
两般春神，一位骑着雄狮，一位乘着凤凰
志趣相投的精灵哟，一起漂洋过海，我的阁下
我们的呼吸是祈祷，我们分享顽童的欢笑

让我们打开礼物——橡籽里的宇宙
让河带我们漂流，一无所求

Wang Ping 王屏

II

Cycad Fossil—a Sonnet Ghazal

for Robert Bjorgum

Let river move us without wants or needs
Let cycads carry their fruit in naked seeds

No flower to adorn your heart, roots pulling
Food from sand, stones. What magic in your seed

White flesh burns the nerves of the ignorant
What desire or love wedged in your coned seed?

Along colored veins—Age of Cycads—rings
Of truths. In your dried palm, an open seed

Naked to sun and moon, herbivores' teeth carry
You across the chasm. In the crown, a seed

Running from pole to pole—the Sea was one
Body, unhinged, spewing lava into your seed

You're not shadows from the Permian of China
Look at this beauty—so simple in your agate seed

铁树

—罗伯特.碧容赠送我世间最珍贵的铁树化石

让河带着我们漂流，一无所求
让铁树的化石打开赤裸的种子

没有花朵装饰你的心房，只有根从沙砾
汲取养分。是什么魔术注入你的种子？

让饱满的果实，最能灼伤无知者的神经
欲望和挚爱，深深地嵌入菠萝状的种子

来自二叠纪的铁树，沿着叶脉圈圈缠绕
历史，在你的手心绽放，干枯的种子

袒露在阳光下，恐龙把你含在口里
穿行地球的板块。花冠上唯一的种子

从南极跋涉到北极——四海本是一体
汪洋，古老的岩浆喷入你的种子

你硕长的阴影，伸过二叠纪盆地
美的如此透明秀丽，玛瑙的种子

Wang Ping 王屏

III

Look at this beauty, so simple in your agate seed
A blue jay calls from the river's blue mouth
What runs from a roof, flows to the East Sea?
What flows from the north, spills into the south?

Last night on the highland, snow and rain
Winter's muddy feet drag behind spring's fawn
In the valley, sounds of a whooping crane
A wheel barrow, copper etched by the dawn

The river has broken the thunder of ice
Swirling boulders, trees, chairs and baby swings
Cottonwood trees swarmed with screeching mice
How the river laughs flying on eagles' wings

Truth can't be buried in the winner's lies
Moon on river's bend, long day of mayflies

心中的河流 THE RIVER WITHIN

美的如此透明秀丽，玛瑙的种子
蓝鸟沿着密西西比河的蓝唇歌唱
哪条大江从地球屋脊直奔东海？
哪条大河从北方漫入墨西哥湾？

昨晚的高原，　雨雪交加
冬日的泥泞拖住春天的小鹿
黑颈鹤的鸣叫，声声断肠
黎明为推车插上青铜翅膀

密西西比河冲破冬天的镣铐
巨石，老树，摇篮狂吐白沫
棉花树顶挂满了尖叫的田鼠
闪流抓起河床，骑上鹰的翅膀

真理再次被胜者的谎言掩盖
河湾的月亮，五月浮寮的爱

Wang Ping 王屏

IV

Moon on river's bend, long day of mayflies
No sound or word from Damascus' desert
Limestone ridge along Silk Route—face of Dubai
Crumbles—wind in hyssop, thyme, wild mustard

This flayed land, so raw, parched, only seeds fly
To take root in the conquerors' footprints
Dusk weeps like sand through hands, pulling first cry
From Azan's throat, a slave sings god's imprints

Home under the ash cloud, darting swallows
Out of hospitals, daisies on smoked walls
Tanks at the border. Shadows at ghettos
Remorse in maze—the last muezzin calls

The Dervish whirls, palm to earth, palm to sky
Who gave us the hand, so humble, so sublime?

心中的河流 THE RIVER WITHIN

河上的月亮,五月浮寮的爱
大马士革的荒漠,没了人迹
石灰岩剥离丝绸之路——破碎的杜拜
只有风,吹过麝香草、野芥末、牛膝

粗砺灼热的土地令人窒息。只有种子
飞翔,在征服者留下的脚印里生根
黄昏的哭泣如沙粒从指缝流出,黑奴
阿匍的第一声祈祷,烙着生命的泪痕

火山的尘土笼罩家乡,燕子飞出
医院,坍塌的土墙爬满荆棘玫瑰
坦克冲出边界,贫民窟阴影徘徊
绵绵的悔恨汇入阿匍最后的召唤

谁向我们伸出双手,如此谦卑、庄严
托钵僧在旋转,一手撑地,一手扶天

Wang Ping 王屏

V

Who gave us the hand, so humble, so sublime?
Which hunter caught the fire in a bird's eye?
My lord, your falcon leads the path of ice and fire
The gate is open for those chosen to climb

The volcano came alive this morning
Glaciers slide into the womb of the earth
How do you stop a heart from trembling
As ice cuts into the fire of new birth

Along the wind path, Knight of thousand hearts
In the East Sea, Maiden of thousand hands
Mist wraps the islands and your boat of glass
The horse calls his master from distant lands

The warrior draws sword from King Arthur's Seat
How do you keep the same, back from the deep?

心中的河流 THE RIVER WITHIN

托钵僧旋转，一手撑地，一手扶天
哪一位猎人在鸟儿的眼里捕捉火焰
阁下，门已打开，等待你的勇士
鹰犬带我们走上冰火交错的山麓

黎明前，火山突然苏醒咳嗽
高耸的冰川滑进大地的子宫
北极长夜，压住生命的烈火
你如何再次启动太阳的脉搏

拥有千心的骑士，沿着风路行走
挥着千手的少女，在东海上漂流
薄雾缠绕着岛屿，掀起玻璃风帆
远方，马嘶嘶地呼唤主人跨鞍

站在亚瑟王的山头，勇士拔剑出鞘
北海深处归来的你，还是那么桀骜

Wang Ping 王屏

VI

in memory of Jan ...

How do you keep the same, back from the deep?
The preserved brain dripping in her gloved hands
All cells are programmed to die—your leap
Of faith, dimpled behind silvery strands
So beautiful, your great love ... what's matter?
Breaths, ladybugs on a sunbathed window
Maverick at crossroad, fish jumping river ...
Is mind matter? The heart, seat of joy and sorrow
Holds stubborn cells. Outside the funeral
Light ripples across sky and prairie grass
Something has taken us by the viscera
A crowd of spirits, darkly, behind the glass

Immortality kills us in the first place
The heart beats alone, keeping its own pace

心中的河流 THE RIVER WITHIN

悼念简

北海深处归来的你，还是那么桀骜
大脑在你的手掌，防腐剂点点滴滴
所有的细胞，没有死亡开关——信仰
大跳跃，银发下的脸，笑靥如玉
你的爱，你的呼吸，还有你的美丽
让瓢虫趴满窗台，接受阳光的记忆
让鱼跳出水、让狂飙徘徊十字路口
意识也算物质吗？我们的心，唯一的
喜悦神。顽固的细胞，总也不肯死去
火葬场外，阳光海浪般滚过天空草地
是什么东西抓住我们的五脏六腑
玻璃门后，幽灵们窃窃私语

追求永生，而首先离去的却是你！
心，为什么如此孤独，如此顽固

Wang Ping 王屏

VII

The heart beats alone, keeping its own pace
Fear, rage, sorrow—storms beyond our range
The river bows and bends, birthing new space
To die and live again—this constant change

Veins of water across the delta wrist, opening
Cupped hands … fish, reeds, frogs mating in puddles
Home … where cranes stop for a drink, then rising
Back to their birthplace. The spirit shuttles

Between heaven and earth—how do you follow
This primordial path? The brain, a wrinkled mass
Keeps us at bay, eyes on the black swallow
From distant sea … messenger through tall grass

Memory split from the Fountain of Youth
You hold us to the place—this beat, this truth

心中的河流 THE RIVER WITHIN

心,为什么如此孤独,如此顽固
恐惧,愤怒,悲哀——心的飓风
河流七里一道弯,制造新的土地
人间的生生死死,何日才能终止

下游的河涨开血管密布的手腕
鱼儿青蛙,在苇塘里跳跃做爱
这就是家乡——仙鹤飞行万里,为了
饮一口出生地的水?精灵们穿梭在

天堂和大地之间。谁能指点迷津
走上原生之路?大脑叠加的灰质
让我们纵横宇宙。看那黑色的海燕
可是穿梭草丛,飞越太平洋的信使?

青春的圣泉,淹没今生前世的记忆
不肯死去的心率,把我们拴在此地

Wang Ping 王屏

VIII

You hold it to this place—this beat, this truth
Wild turkey for guests, yam in sweet rice stuffing
Peacock dance, flamenco hands, sorghum spirits soothe
Strayed ghosts. In China, there's no Thanksgiving
Good words flow from glass to glass. Ten thousand geese
In the sky, ten thousand whales from north to south
Sounds of flute, a pining soul no one can appease
A lover turned into a stone at the river's mouth
A crazed mother, crying for her burst bubble
Breaths of tai chi, circling with phoenix flows
What arrows can silence your fire? A true singer
Soars over the cry of ten thousand crows

We feed ghosts to kill an inherited shame
Nobody claims rivers at the end of game

心中的河流 THE RIVER WITHIN

不肯死去的心率,把我们拴在此地
远方有来客,快捧出火鸡甜酒糯米
孔雀舞,祭神的白酒,吉普赛响板
中国没有感恩节,却富有细语笑颜

从酒杯流向酒杯。天空里飞翔着
一万头野雁,一万海鲸穿越南北
笛声的尾端,一个无法抚慰的精灵
河口处,望乡的女子,在渐渐石化

疯狂的白男,对着消失的泡沫咆哮
呼吸太极,流云钎手如展翅的凤凰
什么箭镞能穿透你的怒火?歌手
穿透群鸦的狂叫,歌声直抵穹苍

我们供奉鬼神,重叙祖先的遗恨
游戏结束后,谁敢再来称霸江河?

Wang Ping 王屏

IX

No one claims rivers at the end of game
Swans trumpet from the head of the Mississippi
Along the trails—snow, dogs, birds—same
Difference as children slide with whoopee
Laugh, and rivers rumble like summer nights
On sandstone bluffs, lovers watch crews dart
Like insects. Walking on water is not a sleight
Of hands but an instinct, echoes of distant stars
And ancient sturgeons upstreaming to go home
Keep going, says the master, one stroke at a time
Breathing between waves, his voice horse, riddled
With tumors, yet he stands, furious and sublime

What arrow points us to grace, here and now?
A swan's touch, his neck bending in a bow

心中的河流 THE RIVER WITHIN

游戏过后,谁敢再来称霸江河?
天鹅的呼唤来自密西西比源头
沿着山路,狗,啄木鸟,积雪
同孩子们呼啸玩耍,滑下山坡

河流呵呵地笑着,加入夏夜狂欢
恋人们坐在砂岩的峭壁,看划艇
昆虫般流动。在水面上行走是本能
不是魔术。沙沙的回响,竟然来自

遥远的太空。回家的路上,鲟鱼不吃
不睡。不许停下,师傅说,一浆一浆
地划,把呼吸定在浪尖。他的声带
被肿瘤挤满,但背影还是如此挺直

温婉的弓,如天鹅颈背,轻柔似水
飞翔的羽箭,直指优美,让我留步

Wang Ping 王屏

X

A swan's touch, neck bending into a bow
A storm without premonition: oaks, pines
Trailers, tents, dreams—all uprooted at night
Everything that should be down in forests is down

Said Ranger Bob, oars dipping like falcons
At dawn the St. Croix unfolds silk ribbons
In the water, clams lure fish, shooting roes
Into their gills, where babies hatch and grow

Our boat cuts the river. Blue turtles bathe in light
Horseflies takes chunks of flesh from our back
Our breaths move with the damselflies—wings
Of butterfly, neon turquoise & shimmering black

We raise our oars to follow summer flood
The river runs through us—our kin, our blood

心中的河流 THE RIVER WITHIN

飞翔的羽箭,直指优美,让我们留步
突袭的风暴不给任何预兆:森林倒地
拖车、木屋、古树、梦想,拦腰截断
"该倒的都已倒下了,护林员鲍勃说

荡起双桨,敏捷如游隼猎鹰的翅膀
水里,河蚌捕捉饿鱼,柔软的吸管
黏住头尾,卵射入鱼鳃,繁衍后代
回家的路上,圣克洛娃河抖开丝带

小船切开水面,没有人声,只有河龟
取暖。马蝇一口就是一块肉,真狠!
我们跟随灯芯蜻蜓呼吸,它们的翅膀
黑似乌金,嵌以宝蓝,更是蝴蝶天使

我们举桨,追逐夏日的炎炎浪情
河流穿过身体—我们的热血,我们的母亲

Wang Ping 王屏

XI

in memory of Todd

The river runs through us—our kin, our blood
Big Dipper, solar winds, life in tannin earth

From Solon Spring to Prescott, 250 miles of flood
We follow clams, milkweeds…odes of same birth

We skid rapids glittered with gold—the stars drape
Around our napes. Namekagen, home for sturgeons

Mahnomen—berries for fish, loons, our daily hearth
Spirits of Minnesota, Wisconsin … In salty streams

We turn boats with boils and eddies, our screams
Echoed by thrushes, tents full of stubborn

Mosquitoes, thunders … dark roast coffee steams
Into the rain, and mist ties the river into a ribbon

We sit, and the world within begins to unravel
As each blade of grass turns with its angel

心中的河流 THE RIVER WITHIN

悼念陶德

河流穿过身体—我们的热血，我们的母亲
北斗星， 太极风， 全部源于红土的生命

锁龙泉到布劳司澋， 250英里的水路
随奶草水蚌奔流， 这就是同源的赞歌

银河挽起独木舟头，顺着金色的河水
漂流。纳姆卡根， 河豚梦中的家乡

野米－鱼和鸭的果子，土著人神圣的主食
明尼苏达，维斯康辛的灵魂，在湿地扎根

小船顺着漩涡飞转， 我们的叫喊
纳入百灵鸟的歌声。帐篷里挤满

蚊子和雷电，咖啡的香味
穿过细雨， 云雾把河流挽成发带

我们静坐，世界在心里缓缓地开放
每一片草叶，都坐着一个天使歌唱

Wang Ping 王屏

XII

Every blade of grass turns with its angel
Every breath we make churns your heartbeat
A child becomes Father's man in the cradle
A wave is a wave regardless of our defeat

A lie bends and bends around the purple night
At twilight the mask unveils a scorched soul
A cycle of 64 days of riches from the Scorpio kite
The way is open, then shuts with a gaping O

The hammer, anvil and stirrup, the smallest bone
In the sea of cochlea, a spiral, a million fingers
Brushing ecstasy to the base of the throne
A ripple is a ripple forever after the seekers

This is the gift I owed you from future and past
This is my eye—blind—in the river wild and fast

心中的河流 THE RIVER WITHIN

每一片草叶,都坐着一个天使歌唱
每一次呼吸,启动我们疲惫的心房
摇篮里的孩子,已长成人类的父亲
我们倒下又站起,前浪挡不住后浪

漫天谎言缠绕紫色的长夜
黎明揭穿失去理性的人兽
齐天的财富来自蝎子风筝
道路张开手,又突然闭口

砧,锤,箍筋,最小的人骨
在耳蜗海里震动,千根手指
不停地把狂喜拨向大脑的根基
波涛追赶波涛,寻觅跟踪寻觅

未来,过去——这是我欠你的补偿
我睁开盲眼,在兽性的河里流荡

Wang Ping 王屏

XIII

This is my eye—blind—in the river wild and fast
Under a steely knee, pleading for a promised freedom

Lies storm, back and forth, between ocean currents
Machines clank to grind her calls for freedom

Not for asylum or paradise, not for money or fame
All she wants is a room in this beautiful country, a freedom

To take children to school, to guide siblings out
Of the maze, to come home in one piece, free

To raise the young, grow old in peace, a place where
Hunger, prison or death can't blackmail freedom

Where the poor, the blind, the small and defeated
Can breathe in dignity. Freedom is never free

Must pave, brick by brick, with eyes and hands
And a heart willing to bleed till it breaks free

心中的河流 THE RIVER WITHIN

我睁开盲眼,在兽性的河里流荡
穿过钢铁凝视,朝着虚诺的自由

谣言刮起飓风,卷起媒体的暗流
雪白机器,碾碎亚裔教授的自由

不为天堂,更不为名利,只想在
美丽的大地,获一席诗歌的自由

传播泥土的真理,把孩子从谎言里摇醒
带他们走出债务的泥潭,重获做人的自由

独立思想行动,欢喜地成长
没有贷款、破产,挟持自由

让穷人、老人,被命运抛弃的小人
都活得尊严。世间没有免费的自由

只有满腔的热血,凝成沙土沥青
一砖一石地铺路,换取一钵自由

Wang Ping 王屏

XIV

A heart willing to bleed until it breaks free
The air drags daggers through our nose and lungs
Across Duluth streets—flash flood, raging trees
At Fort Collins, wrathful gods for our deeds

The spill sprayed with dispersants, black turned white
No flies would lay larvae, rotten ships, reeds …
"We've been eating their evidence!" shouts the fisherman
In his fist, a shrimp with deformed brain, legs & seeds

All the blood wants is flowing to the heart
All the rivers dream is running to the sea
A thousand flags, a thousand hearts and hands
The road ends here, splits like a bird's feet

Please forgive what we made with our greed
Let rivers move without our want or need

心中的河流 THE RIVER WITHIN

一砖一石地铺路,换取一钵自由
燃烧的空气,烘烤烧灼五脏六腑
加州天堂,闪洪,泥石流,大火
神灵的愤怒,降临人间大峡谷

原油溢满墨西哥湾,分散剂腐蚀渔船
芦苇,连苍蝇也不肯在鱼虾上产卵
我们在吃邪恶的证据!瓦德尔先生怒吼
手心一把死虾,癌变的身体,腐烂的头

所有的血,在梦中回归心脏
所有的江河,冥思奔流大海
经幡牵起亿万颗心、亿万双手
密西西比在此分叉,成为鸟足

请原谅我们造就的贪婪星球
让河带我们漂流,一无所有

Wang Ping 王屏

Crown

Let rivers move without our want or need
This beauty—so simple in its agate seed

Moon on river's bend, long day of mayflies
Who gave us the hand, so humble, so sublime?

Our heart keeps beating at its own pace
Back from the deep, how do you keep the same?

You hold us to the place—this beat, this faith
Nobody claims rivers at the end of the game

A swan's touch, neck bending into a bow
The river runs through us—our kin, our blood

Every blade of grass turns with its angel
This is my eye—blind—in the water wild and fast

A heart willing to bleed till it breaks free
My lord, the geese are painting the sky with a V

心中的河流 THE RIVER WITHIN

皇冠

让河带我们漂流,一无所求
玛瑙的种子,如此透明清秀

河湾上的月亮,五月浮寮的爱恋
旋转托钵僧一手撑地,一手扶天

心,为何如此孤独,如此顽固?
桀骜的你,从北海的深处归土

不肯死去的心率,把我们拴在此刻
游戏结束后,谁敢再来称霸江河?

飞翔的羽箭,直指优美,让我们留步
河流穿过身体—我的母亲,我的热血

每一片草叶,都有一个天使歌唱
我睁开盲眼,在兽性的河里流荡

以心,以血,以梦,换一钵自由
我的阁下,野雁把天空画满V勾

注释

1. Lord Charles de Bruce of Scotland: 苏格兰王爷查理斯德布鲁斯,是苏格兰王国创始人罗伯特德布鲁斯的后裔继承人。我们2009年在伦敦机场偶遇,一见如故,成为知己,此组诗是我们多年通信的结果,故献给苏格兰王爷查理斯德布鲁斯。
2. 十四行皇冠: 十四行组诗,每首以上一首的最后一行开头,

Wang Ping 王屏

第十五首取每一行的第一行，挽成皇冠。

3. 罗伯特德布鲁斯是亚瑟王骑士圈的成员。狮子山在爱丁堡大学的后面，我在那儿开诗歌会时，身后的山头不断的招呼我，终于在第三天午餐时，溜出会场，一口气跑上了山顶（那是起码三个小时的路程），那时我不知道此山是亚瑟王和罗伯特德布鲁斯拔剑上马的圣地，两天后，我与查理斯德布鲁斯相遇，他第一个提起的，就是狮子山。

4. 铁树-玛瑙化石：铁树二叠纪时期（3.8亿年前）曾遍布地球，单裸果，种子的肉有毒，通过动物鸟类的食物链，影响神经系统功能。其化石在美国极其珍贵。我的铁树化石是明州最后一位二战老兵赠送的。我的男友带我去看望他爷爷时，他突然从轮椅上抬起头，叫我过去，拍着膝盖说，坐上来。我笑了，拖过椅子坐在他的身旁，我们说了10分钟的话，临走时，他叫他的孙子打开橱柜，拿出化石递给我，说：屏啊，铁树在叫你的名字。

5. 寒冷的北海深处：传说中的神秘之地，亚瑟王和他的骑士乘坐玻璃帆船去探险，寻求不死之泉，归来的骑士寥寥无几。

6. 2010年9月19日，BP石油钻井台在墨西哥湾"鸟足的终端"出事故，泼洒了近五百万桶原油，至今海湾的生态还未恢复，渔民捕捞的鱼虾，都出口，自己不吃，因为都被严重污染，分散剂把原油变成白色小颗粒，生物吃了，基因被改变。瓦德尔先生多方上诉，被当作疯子打回。

7. 密西西比河入墨西哥湾的入口处，形状如鸟足，故称"the End of the Bird's Foot: 鸟足的终端。"此地是瓦德尔先生的家乡，那里原是鱼米之乡，墨西哥湾的虾，以肥美甜嫩著称，畅销全球，尤其是中国。现在海底布满了油管，海面漂满原油，海水漂浮着散发剂的颗粒，生态污染极其严重，瓦德尔先生和他的70岁的妻子以捕虾为生，两人都患癌症，都没有医保。我2012年沿着密西西比河的源头，来到鸟足的终端，找不到旅馆饭店，在码头上遇见瓦德尔先生，他把我带回自己的拖车（穷人住的家），去见他出生在越南的中国妻子，夫妻俩相依为命，虽然穷困，却盛情招待了我三天三夜，成为知己。他们的故事，至今让我唏嘘。

Acknowledgments

Some of the poems have appeared in:

NYT "Story of the Day," *Poetry, New American Writing, Big Scream, Fourth River, Obsidian, Hanging Loose,* and many other journals, a long, shining river of verse around the earth.

Special thanks to

Minneapolis Rowing Club and all the rowers around the world, who love rivers with their hearts and souls;

My immense gratitude to

Jill Mazullo, John Jablonic, Andrej Lawaetz, Kevin Conroy, Philip Johnson, Patty Hansen, Michael Nicholls, Peter Morgan, Scott Armstrong, Jeff Power, Ann Schley, Lynn Randazzo, Jenny Peterson, Bonnie Fuller Kask, Pam Jones ... whose friendship and coaching helped me grow as a rower and person

And Katya and her three amazing children, who transformed my first regatta at the Charles River into a magical wonder ...

And finally, to *New York Times* reporter John Branch and photographer Adam Stoltman, for capturing the magnificent Mississippi in words and images.

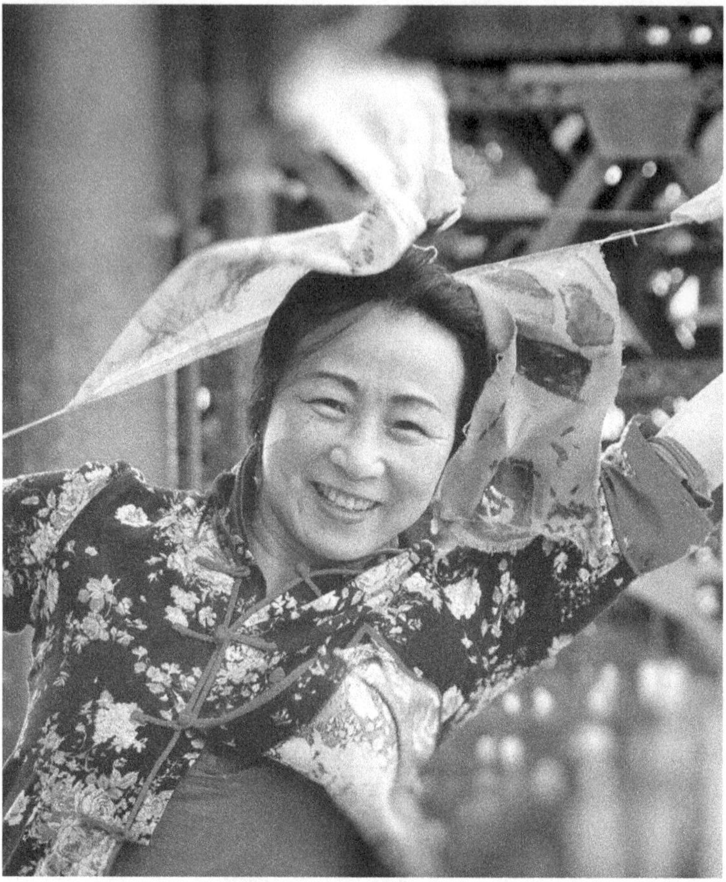

About the Author

DR. PING WANG came from Shanghai and earned her BA at Beijing University and her PhD at NYU. Her books of poetry and prose include *The River Within, My Name Is Immigrant,* and *Life of Miracles along the Yangtze and Mississippi,* among others. She's a recipient of NEA, Bush, Lannan and McKnight Fellowships, AWP Book Award.... She's the director of Kinship of Rivers project, a photographer, dancer and installation artist. Her multimedia installations have been shown at colleges, galleries, museums, river confluences and mountains around the world. She's the Emerita Professor of Poetry at Macalester College.

    wangping.com
    behindthegateexhibit.wangping.com
    kinshipofrivers.org